Other titles by the author

A Different Kind of Teacher
Self-Esteem: The Key to Your Child's Education
The Family: Love It and Leave It
The Power of 'Negative' Thinking
Myself, My Partner

Dedicated to Catherine Ruddle,
whose parenting and teaching put
flesh on the ideas in this book

A DIFFERENT KIND OF DISCIPLINE

A Different Kind of Discipline

Tony Humphreys BA, HDE, MA, PhD

Newleaf

Newleaf
an imprint of
Gill & Macmillan Ltd
Goldenbridge
Dublin 8
with associated companies throughout the world
© Tony Humphreys 1998
0 7171 2807 5

This book is typeset in 11.5pt/13pt Bodoni
Design and print origination by
Carrigboy Typesetting Services, County Cork
Printed by The Guernsey Press

A catalogue record for this book is available
from the British Library.

1 3 5 4 2

CONTENTS

PART I

Introduction

CHAPTER 1

Moving towards True Discipline

❑ *The discipline of old was ill-conceived*
❑ *Popular misconceptions*
❑ *Need for home–school liaison*
❑ *Discipline and person are separate issues*
❑ *Helping victims and perpetrators are*
separate issues
❑ *What discipline is not*
❑ *What discipline is*

❑ *The discipline of old was ill-conceived*

Discipline problems are not a new phenomenon; on the contrary, discipline problems among adults, parents, teachers and clergy have long been commonplace. To say that discipline problems are now more prevalent in homes, schools and communities is accurate to the extent that children are displaying more of these difficult behaviours. But they had good teachers. For decades, parents, teachers and clergy ruled children through fear and intimidation. Behaviours such as shouting, pushing, shoving, beating, hitting, criticising, threatening, ridiculing and scolding were commonplace in homes, schools and churches. Adults who believe that these reactions to children constituted the practice of discipline are sadly misinformed. Such discipline practices were abusive, and whilst they may have fostered quiet in homes and classrooms, they fostered little else of a positive nature. Furthermore, their blocking of the emotional, social and educational development of children had major consequences: many children dreaded failure, lived in fear, were turned off learning and often carried feelings of rage and revenge into their adult lives.

It is not that the adults who perpetrated such ill-disciplined responses towards children wanted deliberately to hurt. But they were members of a religious-dominated culture which believed that human beings were basically flawed and evil and needed to have the badness beaten out and the goodness beaten in. This conceptualisation of the person inevitably fostered 'evil' ways of treating children and, indeed, adults.

Why is it that authoritarianism – which was never desirable – is no longer producing the 'quiet' of old? There are many reasons; most notably that there has been a shift to a pluralist society in which many adults and children are now more educated and more empowered and will no longer accept being dominated and controlled by others.

Proper and humane discipline has never been widely practised. Authoritarianism was and is an act of undisciplined conduct. Those who bemoan its passing are clearly struggling with changing expectations and are in need of help to learn more constructive approaches to discipline. But now there is an opportunity to develop true discipline procedures that rest on the solid foundation of the wonder, value, lovability and capability of human beings. If the old concept of people being 'bad' persists, no real progress will be made in creating order and safety in homes, schools and communities. It is well documented that parents and teachers who love and respect children rarely encounter discipline problems. On the other hand, those who dislike children and who are authoritarian pile up many discipline problems for themselves.

Discipline is not a simple issue but one which demands considerable creativity, commitment, time and resources. It is an issue that many parents and teachers complain about, but one to which they do not give the kind of focus needed.

❏ *Popular misconceptions*

Many parents and teachers see discipline problems solely in terms of under-controlled behaviours such as shouting, hitting, temper tantrums, uncooperative behaviour, back-answering, disruptive actions and so on. This is a very narrow view of the nature of discipline problems and one that is motivated by the need of parents and teachers to have a peaceful and ordered life. If discipline is to be defined as the *practice of care and respect towards others and towards self* then, surely, over-controlled behaviours such as passivity, timidity, shyness, elec-

tive mutism, non-assertiveness and avoidance are as unacceptable as under-controlled actions. Furthermore, if the aim of
discipline systems is to create the emotional and social safety
for each person in the social system (home, school, classroom,
community) to self-actualise, then there needs to be as much
concern for over-controlled behaviour as there tends to be for
under-controlled actions. If under-controlled behaviours block
the development of people, so too do over-controlled reactions.
Ironically, the latter are far more common than the former.
Over-controlled responses have not been targeted by discipline
systems because they do not disrupt, visibly at least, the lives
of others, whereas under-controlled actions do. However, unless discipline systems consider both sets of responses, it is
unlikely that effective discipline will result.

A similar misconception of what constitutes discipline problems is reflected in schools' reactions to bullying behaviour.
Many schools have now developed anti-bullying campaigns.
However, these anti-bullying systems do not target passivity,
and unless there is an equally vigorous anti-passivity campaign,
the anti-bullying mechanisms are unlikely to succeed. Both the
children who bully and those who are victimised need empowerment (Chapter 7) and enhancement of their self-esteem
(Chapter 14). Bullying and passivity are but the opposite sides
of the same coin of emotional and social insecurity. However
it may be reflected, this insecurity needs healing.

A very common misconception of discipline is that it applies
only to children and pupils. It is common to witness teachers
or parents berating children for an under-controlled response
that they themselves frequently employ, for example shouting
or 'put down' remarks. Discipline is as much an issue for
adults as it is for children. Indeed, it is more of a responsibility for adults because children take the cues for many of
their behaviours from adults. The basis of a good discipline
system is adults being in control of themselves (Chapter 11).
This also ensures that double standards – one law for children
and another for adults – do not exist.

A related misconception to the foregoing one is that discipline is about controlling others. It is not the responsibility
of parents and teachers to control children (that is an act of

neglect), but it is their responsibility to help children control themselves. Effective teaching of any behaviour rests on the principle, 'you should practise what you preach'. When parents and teachers regularly lose control with children, they are hardly in a position to demand self-control from children. Furthermore, 'actions always speak louder than words' and children tend to imitate the actions of adults. It is very confusing for children when, on the one hand, adults call for them to be responsible, whilst, on the other hand, the adults themselves abrogate that same responsibility. When teachers and parents lose control, it gives permission to children to act in a similar way and it also gives them the power to control adults. Children have had little responsible power in homes and classrooms, and so any chink in the armour of adults becomes an opportunity to control them.

The basis for an effective discipline system in schools and homes is for both adults and children to learn self-control (Chapter 11).

❑ *Need for home–school liaison*

The most persistent offenders come from troubled homes. Teachers and parents need to be a collective force in creating effective discipline systems in homes and schools. Similar norms, predictability and consistency in applying discipline systems in homes and schools will certainly add to their credibility and durability. Both parents and teachers must not forget that a discipline system is there as much to safeguard children against adults' lack of discipline as it is to safeguard adults' rights in the face of under-controlled behaviour from children.

Particular attention will need to be paid to getting the co-operation of parents who are troubled themselves and may be reluctant to come to any kind of parent–teacher or formal meeting. Equally, a discipline system has to seriously look at means of vindicating the rights of children in the face of adults who continuously violate their rights and of getting those adults confidential professional help.

Nor should teachers have to put up with the minutest violation of their rights in or out of the classroom. It is a failure of a school discipline system when teachers spend more time attempting to control students than teaching them. Of course, neither should students have to tolerate disrespectful behaviour on the part of teachers. And, what is true for teachers and students in the school is also true for parents and children in the home.

The creation, endorsement and commitment to implementation of a just and caring discipline system by parents, teachers and children are the backbone of an effective system. The commitment involves clear communication about the system, predictable and consistent application, fine-tuning of the system as 'weaknesses' emerge, and strong support and cooperation from teachers, principals, management, students and parents. Frequent meetings are essential. Teachers need to back parents in setting up appropriate discipline systems in homes.

A further aspect of the proposed collective responsibility of teachers, parents and children (Chapter 6) is individual empowerment and determination to voice and vindicate their individual rights in schools and homes (Chapter 7).

All the parties to the establishment of discipline systems need to look at ways of preventing discipline problems (Chapter 12). A major aspect of preventing discipline problems is the recognition that all discipline starts with self (Chapter 11). A further important dimension of prevention is the nature of interrelationships between all those in positions of authority.

When discipline problems do occur, it is the discipline system that has failed rather than the people involved. Resolution of violated needs lies in finding and correcting the weaknesses in the system. However, a system is only as strong as its members. Individuals may need help for their under-controlled or over-controlled responses but the provision of such aid must be seen as a separate issue to that of the vindication of the rights of victims (see below).

❏ *Discipline and person are separate issues*
Whether or not the home or school or community develops an appropriate discipline system very much depends on the way the person is viewed. If human beings are seen as 'bad' or 'evil' or 'stupid' or 'slow', order and harmony cannot be

achieved in homes, schools and communities. If the person of each parent, teacher and child is regarded as unique and sacred and of immense value and worth, then there exists a solid foundation for effective discipline.

Discipline is part and parcel of human relationships and it is vital to see it within that dynamic social process. Unconditional love, acceptance and affirmation of a person's vast intellectual potential correspond to the deepest longings, not only of every child, but of every adult as well. When the fundamental needs of human beings are enshrined in a discipline system, the cornerstone for an effective system has been well and truly laid.

What follows from this philosophy is that the person of each child, teacher and parent must not be threatened by any one bit of troublesome behaviour. Certainly, the difficult behaviour has to be confronted in order to restore the rights of victims that may have been violated, but this must be done in a way that leaves intact the self-esteem of both victim and perpetrator. It is implicit in this way of responding to undisciplined conduct that no relationship – whether between adults and children, adults and adults, principals and teachers or parents and teachers – must be broken because of either socially inappropriate actions or lack of appropriate actions. The aims must be threefold: maintain respect for the victim's and the perpetrator's person; maintain the relationship; and take clear and firm corrective action on the specific behaviour that has upset the equilibrium of the home, classroom or community.

Discipline is not just about what happens between people, such as parents and children, children and teachers, teachers and teachers – it is equally about what happens within people. Indeed, the latter is often a major determinant of the former. Many students, teachers and parents carry the emotional baggage of their own poor sense of lovability and capability into their respective roles. Unless there is great emphasis on caring for people (Chapter 15) and there are structures that can be availed of for healing inner hurts, discipline systems will fail in schools and homes.

Discipline has nothing to do with controlling disruptive or other unacceptable behaviours, whether on the part of children or adults. It has everything to do with ensuring a safe and valuing environment so that the rights and needs of people are respected, vindicated and safeguarded. Within the home, school and community each adult and child has the right to be loved, valued, seen for self, communicated with in open, respectful and equalising ways, and allowed to pursue legitimate work, leisure, spiritual and other goals in life. When such interactions are not present, it is incumbent on the members of the social system – be it the home, school or community – to devise structures that guard these basic human rights. Unfortunately, few such structures exist at present.

❏ *Helping victims and perpetrators are separate issues*

There has been an unfortunate tendency to enmesh the issues of victims with those of perpetrators. This enmeshment has too often meant that the rights of victims of ill-discipline are neglected. When a discipline problem arises, the primary action that needs to be taken is the reinstatement of the violated rights of the victim. This is what a discipline system is all about. Only when this has been established can the focus be shifted to helping the perpetrator. All perpetrators are victims themselves and the concern must be to discover and resolve the underlying causes of aggressive or passive behaviour when it occurs. This issue goes beyond discipline (Part V) and must not be confused with discipline procedures (Parts III and IV).

❏ *What discipline is not*

When discipline is employed with a view to controlling others it is unlikely to be successful. It may but generally will not achieve quietness, and it will not heal the aggressive or passive behaviours that led to the blocking of the needs of others. It certainly will not promote the ultimate goal of discipline, which must be mutual respect and caring between all the members of a social system.

Many teachers who spend the bulk of their time in the classroom attempting to control the unruly behaviour of pupils complain that all their efforts have little effect on the children; many parents have similar complaints. These discipline efforts tend to be authoritarian and aggressive in nature and are doomed to failure because they do not encapsulate the basic respect for another human being that adults would want for themselves.

When adults employ methods of control that are aggressive, dominating, cynical, sarcastic or manipulative, they are attempting to fight fire with fire and are being 'abusive' in ways similar to those of the children they are attempting to control. These strategies produce only more ill-disciplined reactions and a vicious cycle may now be created.

❏ *What discipline is*

Discipline is about safeguarding the rights of people who are exposed to uncooperative, aggressive or other blocking responses on the part of others. Such safeguarding mechanisms are needed in homes, schools, workplaces and communities, and are needed in response to adults' as much as to children's under-controlled or over-controlled behaviour. An essential principle underpinning the approach of this book is that people are responsible for the fulfilment of their own needs and that the socially difficult behaviours of others must not block them from having their needs met. A second principle is that ill-disciplined actions are not designed to hurt or block another but are genuine attempts on the part of the perpetrators to get their own blocked needs met or to prevent experiences of failure, hurt and rejection. These themes will be elaborated throughout the book.

Taking cognisance of these two principles, this book will explore alternative and more effective ways of responding to under-controlled and over-controlled behaviours. Responses that are more likely to be successful need to include consideration of the following factors:

- Homes, schools and communities must be involved in the creation and maintenance of discipline systems.
- Discipline is primarily about safeguarding the rights of victims of under-controlled or over-controlled behaviours to be valued, respected and allowed pursue legitimate life goals (Chapter 5).
- There must be a genuine desire to understand why perpetrators are engaging in undesirable behaviours (Chapter 4).

- There must be clear indications that discipline responses are attempts to maintain solidly the rights of those at the receiving end of socially difficult behaviours. It follows from this that the way responses are phrased and acted upon are essential to the clear communication of their message (Chapter 5).

- Reciprocal responsibility – between teachers and children, teacher and teacher, leaders and teachers, parents and children, and parents and teachers – is basic to the meeting of needs (Chapter 6).

- Safeguarding structures which uphold and vindicate, when violated, the rights of children, parents and teachers must be developed (Chapters 8, 9 and 10).

- Active means to empower all members of homes, schools and communities to stand up for their rights must be created (Chapter 7).

- Safeguarding structures must be directly and clearly communicated to all members of homes and schools as well as to relevant and influential agencies outside the targeted systems.

- When sanctions are employed, the aim must be to demonstrate to perpetrators the strong determination of the home, school or community to maintain and reinstate the violated rights of victims.

- There must be commitment to prevention of discipline problems (Chapter 12).

- There must be recognition that prevention is aided by self-control (Chapter 11).

- Structures that go beyond discipline must be created to help perpetrators (and victims) resolve their personal vulnerabilities or difficult relationships (Chapter 14).

- Strong reinforcement of responsible behaviours of children, people in authority and parents must be integral to devising appropriate discipline and 'beyond discipline' systems.

- A philosophy of care must be developed in homes and schools so that each member feels cherished (Chapter 15).

This book aims at creating effective discipline systems and healing systems that go beyond discipline in homes, schools and communities. It sees that the partnership of homes and schools is central. Part II of the book, 'The Discipline Problem', describes what constitutes and causes discipline problems (Chapters 2 and 3), and shows how discipline problems are cries for help (Chapter 4). Part III, 'Discipline is about Safeguarding Rights', sets out the rights and responsibilities of children, parents and teachers (Chapters 5 and 6), empowering procedures for children, parents and teachers (Chapter 7) and safeguarding structures required to uphold and vindicate the rights of victims (Chapters 8–10). Part IV, 'Prevention and Intervention', examines prevention of discipline problems (Chapters 11 and 12) and what to do when things go wrong (Chapter 13). Part V, 'Beyond Discipline', deals with responding to the cries for help of perpetrators (Chapter 14) and the creation of caring homes and schools (Chapter 15).

This book is a manual for everybody to set up caring and effective discipline systems in homes, schools and communities. It has direct relevance for all parents, parent groups, community groups, educators, school managers, boards of management, teachers' unions, school inspectors and government.

PART II

The Discipline Problem

CHAPTER 2

What are Discipline Problems?

❑ *Discipline problems*
❑ *Discipline problems in the home*
   ■ Discipline problems of parents
   ■ Discipline problems of children
❑ *Discipline problems in the school*
   ■ Discipline problems of students
   ■ Discipline problems of teachers

❑ *Discipline problems*

This chapter examines those discipline problems that typically arise in the home and in the school. Discipline problems occur when the presence of certain behaviours (under-controlled reactions) or the absence of certain behaviours (over-controlled reactions) jeopardises the rights and needs of others and, possibly, of the perpetrators themselves. Of course, this undisciplined conduct may be exhibited not only by children but also by adults. The target of those who employ under-controlled reactions is to control others, whilst the target of those who use over-controlled reactions is to control self, but in a way that blocks their own rights and needs. Accordingly, the aims of discipline systems will be to take care of the victims of under-controlled discipline problems and to empower the person who displays over-controlled reactions.

❑ *Discipline problems in the home*

Parents can expect too much of children and too little of themselves in terms of disciplined behaviours. Parents would do well to understand that children learn most of their undisciplined conduct from them or other significant adults in the family. What parents 'give out' in terms of undisciplined behaviour is likely what they will get back.

■ Discipline problems of parents

Discipline problems can be categorised into under-controlled and over-controlled reactions. Parents who engage in under-controlled behaviours, a list of which is given below, do so out of their own low self-esteem and insecurities; whilst they have no intention of hurting their children, the fact is that hurt is what their children experience. Unless parents get to the source of their under-controlled actions, they are unlikely to change those behaviours that are devastating to their children's overall development.

Parents' under-controlled discipline problems
<ul><li>Shout at children</li><li>Order, dominate and control children</li><li>Use sarcasm and cynicism as means of control</li><li>Ridicule, scold and criticise children</li><li>Label children as 'bad', 'bold', 'stubborn', 'stupid', 'lazy', 'no good'</li><li>Threaten that they will leave</li><li>Threaten to send children away</li><li>Physically threaten children</li><li>Physically assault children</li><li>Push, pull and shove children</li><li>Assign punishments out of proportion to misdemeanours</li></ul> <ul><li>Compare children to one another</li><li>Have an obvious favourite in the family</li><li>Do not call children by their first names</li><li>Are too strict</li><li>Expect too much of children</li><li>Show no interest in children's welfare</li><li>Punish mistakes and failures</li><li>Never apologise for being wrong</li><li>Do not say 'please' and 'thank you' to children</li><li>Are inconsistent and unpredictable in response to children's irresponsible behaviours</li><li>Withdraw love from children</li></ul>

As a therapist I have helped mothers who for years 'put up' with being terrorised by their partners and did not stand up for the children when their father perpetrated the same physical and verbal violence on them. These children did not feel loved by either their father or their mother. Both had failed in parenting. The passivity of the mother resulted in as much neglect of the children as did the father's aggression. For too long the aggressive parent – whether father or mother – has been seen as the 'devil' and the passive parent as the 'martyr' or 'saint'. It is much more accurate to say that both the aggressive and the passive parent are engaging in undisciplined conduct and are failing to parent properly.

Parents' over-controlled discipline problems	
• Allow the partner control self and children	• Let children slide out of responsibility
• Spoil and overindulge children	• Use children as a go-between in relationship with partner
• Use hostile silences to control children and partner	
• Sulk and withdraw	• Are highly dependent on partner and children for affection and recognition
• Rarely express needs	
• Rarely say 'no'	• Are timid and fearful
• Do not 'rock the boat'	• Avoid challenges
• Give in too easily to unreasonable requests	• Are conformist
	• Are perfectionistic
• Do not stand up for self and children when physically or emotionally abused	• Accept undesirable behaviours from children
	• Do too much for children
• Attempt to please all the time	• Overprotect children
	• Have an overwhelming desire to be wanted
• Avoid contentious issues	

Parents who engage in over-controlled behaviours have not yet learned to parent themselves, and until this disciplined caring of themselves begins, they are not in a place to discipline and be unconditionally loving towards their children.

▪ Discipline problems of children

The family culture is the most powerful influence on children. The nature of parents' interactions with and reactions to each other and their children will largely determine whether children become mainly disciplined or undisciplined. Generally speaking, children tend to identify more strongly with one of their parents and will repeat that parent's behavioural characteristics or will be diametrically opposite. When parents engage in either under-controlled or over-controlled responses, children in turn will present with discipline problems.

Children's under-controlled discipline problems	
• Nail-biting	• Play truant from school
• Hyperactivity	• Attention-seeking
• Impulsiveness	• Argumentative
• Mischievousness	• Disruptive of other family members' activities
• Carelessness about homework	• Act tough
• Overexcitability	• Hostile reactions to reasonable criticism
• Uncontrolled laughter or giggling	• False accusations of parents
• High distractibility	• Temper tantrums
• Speak too fast	• Aggressive outbursts in response to reasonable requests
• Destructiveness of own or other family members' property	• Unwillingness to share domestic chores
• Defacing of books	• Bully siblings
• Use of vulgar or obscene language	• Tease siblings
• Frequent minor delinquencies	• Dominate and control siblings
• Do not listen	• Frequent physical fights with siblings or peers
• Hate school	• Regular complaints that other children do not like them
• Blame others for mistakes and failures	• Frequent relaying of 'dirty' stories
• Highly critical of others	• Overinterest in sexual matters
• Boastful	
• Show off	

Parents are much more likely to complain about children who engage in under-controlled behaviour than about those children who express their dissatisfaction with family life by means of over-controlled reactions.

When children exhibit over-controlled discipline problems, they tend to be either avoiders or compensators. The avoiders want to slide out of any home, social or school activity that threatens them. On the other hand, children who compensate overwork at the activities that threaten them. Hence these children can be those who constantly please parents in the home, are overeager to please relatives and other visitors to the home and are the 'perfect' students in school. Many parents and teachers misinterpret these children's compensatory over-controlled behaviours as evidence of high self-esteem but the sad reality is that these children dread rejection and failure and do anything in their power to offset these threatening experiences.

Children's over-controlled discipline problems	
• Extreme shyness • Poor or no self-confidence • Strong tendency to remain alone • School 'phobic' • Timidity • Fearfulness of new challenges • Mutism • Avoidance of games • Tendency not to mix with other children • Overstudious • Frequent day-dreaming • Worrying unduly • Poor motivation to learn • Appear 'lost in another world' • Obsessional or compulsive behaviours • Overly exact	• Meticulous • Undue anxiety over school examinations • Undue distress over failures and mistakes • Perfectionistic • Overabsorption in hobby or interest • Hypersensitive • Little or no eye contact • Few or no requests for help • Nervous when answering questions • Poor response to affirmation and praise • Wanting to please all the time • Fading into background when brothers or sisters are present

Children's discipline problems are peculiar to their home situation and have to be seen, understood and responded to within that unique culture.

❑ *Discipline problems in the school*

Typically, teachers view only under-controlled actions as discipline problems because these actions can seriously disrupt their classes. However, teachers must recognise that over-controlled behaviour can also have detrimental effects, not necessarily on classroom order, but on students' emotional, social and educational development. Teachers must also accept that they too can exhibit over-controlled responses to stressful situations and that their lack of action can add to classroom disorder, increase their own stress levels, lower their level of self-esteem and cause strain in staff relationships.

Students' over-controlled responses must be as much a cause for concern as are under-controlled responses. The lack of discipline behaviour shown by over-controlled students, principally towards themselves, needs to be corrected so that they can resume again a welfare path.

Examples of under-controlled discipline problems on the part of students and teachers are shouting, insolence, verbal aggression, physical aggression and sarcasm. Instances of over-controlled discipline problems which again may be enlisted by both students and teachers include passivity, people-pleasing, avoidance of confrontation, timidity, fearfulness and elective mutism.

The effects of both types of discipline problems will be determined by their frequency, intensity and duration in terms of both the length of time the particular behaviour lasts in the immediate situation (seconds, minutes, hours) and the length of time it has been presenting (days, weeks, years).

Some of the possible effects of discipline problems in the classroom are:

- Disruption of classroom order
- Disruption of the perpetrator's own learning (or teaching)
- Disruption of other students' learning

- Physical, emotional, social and intellectual distress to other students
- Physical, emotional, social and intellectual distress to teacher
- Increased stress levels of teacher
- Disruption of other classes that overhear the under-controlled reaction of the student or teacher
- Damage to teacher's or student's property

Physical distress arises where the victim (student or teacher) is pushed, shoved, pulled or hit. Emotional distress arises where the victim is called names, 'put down', sneered at or humiliated. Social distress arises from the public nature of some discipline problems where the victim feels embarrassed or ashamed; nobody, neither student nor teacher, wants to lose face in front of others. Intellectual distress arises when remarks are made about intelligence, when labels such as 'fool' or 'stupid' are used, or when failures or mistakes are laughed at or ridiculed.

■ Discipline problems of students

When examining the discipline problems of students there must be no intention to blame or judge, but only to highlight that such behaviours cannot be allowed to block the development of others. Indeed, as will be seen, students who perpetrate difficult behaviours are themselves victims of the problematic behaviours of others. The examples of under-controlled and over-controlled discipline problems given below are indicative of the kinds of discipline problems that teachers experience.

Students' under-controlled discipline problems	
In classroom	• Turn around in class
	• Talk out of turn in class
• Enter room noisily	• Rock in chairs
• Push and shove other students	• Walk around classroom without permission
• Shout out to others	• Talk and mutter to themselves
• Bang desk on sitting down	• Distract others
• Try to be funny	

- Lift desk with knees
- Start singing or humming
- Make distracting verbal or physical noises
- Constantly fidget with apparatus
- React aggressively to appropriate feedback
- Throw missiles around class
- Interfere with other students' work
- Tease and taunt other students
- Have temper outbursts
- Steal other students' possessions
- Make irrelevant comments
- Damage other students' or teacher's property
- Abscond from classroom
- Are late for classes
- Break rules regarding school uniform etc.
- Engage in general rowdiness or horseplay
- Make cheeky or impertinent remarks
- Verbally abuse teacher or other students
- Physically threaten teacher or other students
- Physically assault teacher or other students

Outside classroom
- Bully other students
- Show lack of concern for others
- Break rule of no smoking
- Leave school grounds without permission
- Race along school corridors
- Are unruly while waiting
- Use vulgar language
- Make rude gestures at teachers or other students
- Verbally abuse teachers or other students
- Loiter in restricted areas
- Give cheeky or impertinent responses to teachers or other students
- Are destructive of school property
- Physically threaten teachers or other students
- Physically assault teachers or other students

This list is not exhaustive. Each teacher needs to make a list of the problems that occur in and outside the classroom so that appropriate actions can be taken to reinstate order, harmony and mutual respect in the classroom and school premises.

Students' over-controlled discipline problems	
In classroom	• Poor or no spontaneous participation in class
• Extreme shyness	• Overattachment to class teacher
• Timidity	• No requests for help
• Fearful of new situations	• No eye contact
• Elective mutism	• Extreme nervousness when answering questions
• Excessive academic efforts	• Irrelevant answers to questions
• Frequent day-dreaming	• Frequent breaking-off of speech in the middle of a sentence
• Worry unduly	• Work avoidance
• Poor motivation to learn	• No contact with other students
• Appear 'lost in another world'	
• Obsessional or compulsive	*Outside classroom*
• Overexact	• Remain alone
• Meticulous	• Avoid school games
• Undue anxiety over academic performance	• Stay apart at break times
• Undue silent distress over mistakes or failures	• Have no friends
• Preoccupation with scholastic results	• Are absent from school events
• 'Perfect' student	
• Poor response to recognition and praise	
• Failure to respond when addressed	

It can be seen that students who engage in over-controlled responses do not disrupt significantly the lives of others, but they are highly at risk and urgently need help.

The prevalence of both sets of discipline problems differs from school to school and area to area. It is the task of each school to assess its own level of discipline problems and to set about developing a caring discipline system wherein the dignity and rights of all members of the school are valued and vindicated.

■ Discipline problems of teachers

An issue that teachers must face is that they themselves can and do exhibit both kinds of discipline problems. Acceptance of and a willingness to take responsible action on this fact will alone go some way towards resolving discipline problems in schools.

Teachers' under-controlled discipline problems	
• Shout at students	• Do not like some students
• Order, dominate and control students	• Have obvious favourites
• Employ cynicism and sarcasm as means of control	• Do not know students' first names
	• Do not call students by their first names
• Ridicule, scold, criticise	• Are too strict
• Label students as 'dull', 'weak', 'lazy', etc.	• Are impatient with students who are slow in understanding a lesson
• Physically threaten students	
• Glare at students	• Expect too much of students
• Push and shove students	• Punish mistakes and failures
• Are violent towards students	
• Give extra schoolwork or 'lines' as punishments	• Are inconsistent and unpredictable in response to difficult behaviour
• Are dismissive of students	• Are rude to students
• Never apologise for mistakes	• Leave classroom half-way through a lesson
• Pass on to next lesson without regard to students who have not mastered first lesson	• Are moody
	• Humiliate students
	• Waste time
• Compare one student to another	• Are not prepared for lessons
• Are judgmental	• Do not say 'please' and 'thank you' to students

When teachers engage in these behaviours they do so not to deliberately hurt children but because of their own hidden insecurities. Nevertheless, the effects on students' well-being are devastating. Furthermore, these teachers are hardly in a position to request students to be 'in-control' when they practise the opposite.

Students can spot that teachers who exhibit over-controlled discipline problems pile up as many classroom problems for themselves as do their colleagues who exhibit under-controlled discipline problems. The lack of action by passive teachers leads to obvious personal frustration and strain. Students quickly detect that teachers who are passive and lack firmness can be controlled by them and they can make the lives of such teachers intolerable.

Teachers' over-controlled discipline problems	
• Are shy and reserved • Are passive • Are timid • Are overanxious to please • Have difficulty saying 'no' • Are perfectionistic • Hate change • Want students to like them • Fear students • Worry how colleagues view them • Allow students to get away with undesirable behaviours • Do not disclose classroom management problems • Overwork on preparation of lessons	• Do not confront other teachers or leaders on unacceptable actions • Are apathetic (have given up trying) • Are unpredictable and inconsistent • Lack firmness • Want high academic results • Avoid staffroom • Stay silent at staff meetings • May gossip but at one remove • Worry unduly about examination results • Are overdedicated to teaching

CHAPTER 3

The Causes of Discipline Problems

- ❏ *The cause signifies the 'cure'*
- ❏ *Causes arising from home*
- ❏ *Causes arising from within children*
- ❏ *Causes arising from peers*
- ❏ *Causes arising from teachers*
- ❏ *Causes arising from staff relationships*
- ❏ *Causes arising from school leadership*
- ❏ *Causes arising from school environment*
- ❏ *Causes arising from outside home and school*

❏ *The cause signifies the 'cure'*

The ultimate means of resolving discipline problems is to identify and address their causes. However, alongside the focus on the perpetrator, there has to be equal consideration of the distress of the victims of undisciplined conduct. It can take considerable time, resources, expertise, patience and endurance to resolve why people act in difficult ways, and in the meantime the question has to be: who takes care of the welfare of the victims? Whilst it is acknowledged that the vulnerabilities of perpetrators of under-controlled or over-controlled responses require and deserve healing (because all perpetrators are victims themselves), alongside this, discipline procedures must be developed to safeguard and reinstate the violated rights of victims. Caring for the perpetrators of undisciplined conduct is a separate issue from safeguarding the rights of victims and goes beyond the discipline systems that are needed in schools, homes and communities. What is proposed is the creation of a two-tier system: a discipline system which cares for victims and does not violate the rights of perpetrators and another system which goes beyond discipline and focuses on per-petrators, and healing the causes of their discipline problems, without jeopardising the welfare of others.

Whoever may exhibit the undisciplined behaviour – children or adults – getting to its cause is an essential aspect of the 'beyond discipline' procedures needed in homes, schools and communities (see Part V). The causes of discipline problems may be found within the home, within the school or within the community.

Not all the discipline problems of children are due to difficult home circumstances. The school system itself and the difficult behaviours of teachers can also be the source of children's problematic responses. Of course, peer influences and actions are yet another source. Equally, not all the problematic behaviours of teachers are by-products of their personal vulnerabilities, but can be precipitated by external factors such as poor leadership, neglectful educational system, underresourced school, alienating staff environment, overemphasis on academic results, overcrowding in classrooms, overly large class and undue pressures from parents, churches, media and governments.

The most common cause of discipline problems is that people react (rather than 'proact') to the under-controlled or over-controlled behaviour of another. This is a case where aggression breeds aggression, or passivity and indecisiveness breed frustration and intolerance. In such reactive situations both parties become perpetrators of undisciplined conduct and there exists no forum for resolution of differences. There are underlying reasons why this scenario occurs frequently and these, generally, lie in the realms of self-esteem, personal vulnerability and co-dependent relationships.

The resolution of discipline problems lies primarily in addressing their specific causes. This can be a complex, time-consuming but necessary exercise and, depending on the particular causes, can involve the cooperation of a number of individuals and social systems. The different sources of discipline problems in schools and homes are identified in the following sections.

❑ Causes arising from home

Some children are house 'angels' (over-controlled) and school 'devils' (under-controlled), whilst others are house 'devils' and school 'angels'. There are also children who are 'angels' or 'devils' both at home and in school. The causes of these reactions lie primarily in how parents relate to each other and to their children and how children relate to each other. Parents can vary greatly in their responses to individual children: the common assumption that all children within the one family are reared the same is inaccurate. The main causes of discipline problems in the home that are commonly carried into the school are:

- Poor self-esteem of parents
- Poor relationship between parents
- Poor relationships between parents and children
- Loss of parent through death, separation, desertion or divorce
- Undesirable behaviours of parents
- Lack of continuous relationship with one parent in the first three years of life
- Modelling by parents of socially unacceptable behaviours (idleness, irritability, passivity, drunkenness, drug abuse and so on)
- Poor parenting skills
- Subcultural background whose values, morals and standards differ from those of the larger culture into which children have to fit as they grow up
- Rivalry and hostility between siblings

Most of these causes need little elaboration. As regards self-esteem, parents cannot give children what they have not got themselves and those who have self-esteem difficulties pass these on to their children. Typical self-esteem difficulties of parents are lack of love of self, lack of confidence, dependence on others for approval, addiction to work or success, and fear of failure.

The relationship between parents is also important to children as they depend on both parents (where there are two) for love and security and become very troubled when parents relate to each other in hostile ways, when there is violence or when there are unrelenting silences or frequent arguments.

The major source of children's discipline problems is how their parents relate to them. When parents are dominating, controlling, hypercritical or grossly neglectful, then children become deeply insecure and will manifest their feelings of rejection through problematic behaviours.

Poor parenting skills can lead to the development of a host of problematic responses from children. These children are feverishly searching for boundaries that will provide them with some level of security. Parenting is not an instinctive skill. Human behaviour is far too complex psychologically and socially for parents or teachers to rely on biological instincts and drives.

Children who come from a subculture will quickly notice the differences between them and their peers from the larger culture, and their peers, too, will notice the differences. These differences can become sources of anxiety and insecurity for the subculture children and weapons to be used by some of the larger culture children. The discipline problems arising between 'townies' and children from rural areas are familiar to teachers and parents.

❏ *Causes arising from within children*

It is important to keep in mind that the personal sources of each individual's discipline problems are unique to that person's biographical history. When children come to school they may carry within them vulnerabilities that can lead to them being under-controlled or over-controlled in their behaviour:

- Poor self-esteem
- Poor knowledge levels
- Poor motivation to learn
- Developmental delays
- Physical or mental disability

The most common cause of discipline problems arising within children themselves is not feeling good about themselves. When students see themselves as unlovable or lacking capability, they will act in ways that accord with these feelings about themselves. Until such students' images of themselves change, they are doomed to making life difficult for themselves and others.

Children may have low knowledge and motivational levels when they come from homes where reading, stimulation, education, language development and skills for independent living are not strongly present or valued. These children will conform much more to the low expectations of home rather than the more realistic ones of school. It can be too threatening for children to rise above parents' expectations. These children will be at a serious disadvantage when they come to school and go into other social situations and may, as a consequence, suffer ridicule or criticism, which can precipitate aggressive or withdrawal reactions from them.

Some children may have experienced developmental delays, and when they go to school, they may have poorer physical coordination and poorer reading and language abilities and, overall, may be markedly different in behaviour from their peers. The children themselves may become self-conscious about these differences, but the situation is made even worse if teachers or other students criticise, ridicule or bully them. Such responses will affect the victims' self-esteem, and consequently emotional, social and more learning difficulties will arise.

Some students have mental or physical disabilities, whether from brain damage, chromosomal aberrations or other unknown reasons. At least one-third of these children also experience psychological and social difficulties. The new educational policy of having students with moderate to mild disability attend mainstream schools has put extra pressures on teachers; in such circumstances teachers may lose control and some of the other students may exploit the teacher's distraction.

Children on either prescribed or non-prescribed drugs can be moody, aggressive, restless, drowsy or withdrawn. The number of children being prescribed tranquillisers and antidepressants is a worrying phenomenon. What children require is solutions for their discipline problems, not symptomatic treatments, which, in the long run, only exacerbate these problems.

Not all of the causes of discipline problems arising within children are brought into the school from home; the school staff can cause inner conflicts in students. Examples include:

- Fear of teachers
- Fear of examinations
- Fear of standing up and speaking in class

Teachers who are feared by students display a range of undisciplined behaviours that seriously damage students' self-esteem: criticism, dominance, sarcasm, cynicism, ridicule, scolding, impatience, intolerance, authoritarianism, irritability, and verbal and physical aggression. All of these responses precipitate either aggression or withdrawal and silent resentment on the part of the victimised students and they are always emotionally disruptive. Students who are passive and quiet get hurt, those who are verbally quick 'talk back' and those who are hostile make scenes.

Fear of examinations is an all too common source of discipline problems. Its effects are well known: anxiety, anger, temper outbursts, concentration problems, memory difficulties, insomnia, headaches, muscle tension, mental blocks, depression, dropping out of school and even suicide. This fear comes from too great a pressure on children for examination performance by parents or teachers or both.

Some students, particularly in adolescence, have a fear of standing up and speaking in class. This may stem from sensitivity over height or voice change or fear of making a fool of themselves. If teachers are insensitive to this difficulty, discipline problems are a likely result.

❏ *Causes arising from peers*

The literature on bullying has highlighted the effect that the under-controlled behaviours of students can have on their victims. Generally speaking, boys tend to be more direct in bullying: pushing, shoving, name calling, taunting, beating up, hostile teasing, intimidating, defacing their victims' schoolwork, ostracising, stealing. Girls tend to employ a more indirect form of bullying but one which can be just as vicious and damaging of their victims' self-esteem and their physical, social, intellectual and emotional safety. Indirect bullying may involve gossiping about the victim, sending insulting notes about the victim around the school, ignoring or ostracising the victim, and giggling and laughing when the victim is present.

Academic and, indeed, sports competition between children can be a cause of discipline problems among students who are threatened by the achievements of others. Such students may resort to all types of behaviour either to outdo or to thwart competitors. A teacher once told me about his eight-year-old son who was discovered to have short-sightedness. The child was duly brought to an optician and appropriate spectacles were prescribed but no improvement in the eyesight occurred. The child was then referred to a consultant optician who, after testing the child's eyes, asked a wise question: 'What child is this boy sitting next to in class?' The boy happened to be sitting next to the highest achiever in the class. Being the teacher's son, this was emotionally and intellectually threatening for him and, unconsciously, the child developed the sight problem so that expectations of him would be reduced. How marvellously clever! The consultant advised that the boy be seated next to a less competitive child; he could also have advised that the pressure for academic performance should be reduced within the child's family. In any case, some months after the change of seating, the child's sight returned to normal. The story is an example of an over-controlled response to a threatening situation; only for the consultant's insight, this child would have been doomed to poor sight and poor academic attainment.

Peer influence can also play a strong role in bringing about difficult behaviours in children. A frequent observation is that children who show high academic potential in primary school within a short time do far less well in secondary school. These students may fear being seen as a 'swot' or 'teacher's pet', and in order not to suffer rejection by their peer group, they conform to its norms of avoidance of learning, 'going for the average' and disruption of classes. These children have low self-esteem and their need to be accepted by their peers is stronger than that of students with a higher sense of self. Peer influence in terms of drug experimentation, playing truant, victimisation of teachers or other students and planned efforts to disrupt class or school order are other causes of discipline problems.

The leaders of these activities tend to be poor academically and achieve recognition through being the 'hard man' or 'ringleader' or 'one up on teachers'. They also have quite profound self-esteem difficulties.

❑ *Causes arising from teachers*

There is no doubt that teachers can be their own worst enemies when it comes to creating classroom discipline problems. Very often it is teachers' own lack of self-control or passivity that triggers similar responses from students. The causes lie in the emotional baggage that teachers carry with them into the classroom and staffroom:

- Poor self-esteem
- Dependence on academic performance
- Dependence on approval of colleagues, parents and sometimes students
- Marital difficulties
- Hatred of teaching
- Dislike of children
- Burn-out
- Apathy
- Rigidity
- Competition with other teachers
- Fear of failure
- Feelings of being socially or intellectually inferior to other teachers
- Resentment and bitterness over not gaining promotion
- Alienation from colleagues
- Dread of change
- Work addiction
- People-pleasing
- Doubts about teaching competence
- Poor physical health

Any of these issues can precipitate undisciplined behaviours.

❏ *Causes arising from staff relationships*

Staff relationships are a major source of pressure for teachers and can lead to loss of control or 'anything for a peaceful life' responses. Schools need to place more emphasis on and give more time and resources to creating staff relationships that are healthy, open, cooperative, cohesive and dynamic. The causes of staff problems may lie within teachers themselves or in the lack of structures or behaviours that promote good staff relationships:

- Infrequent staff meetings
- Lack of consultation
- Little or no group decision-making
- Authoritarian or manipulative or passive leadership
- Cliques
- Lack of support
- Non-availability of leaders or colleagues
- Unapproachable leaders or colleagues
- Poor level of social interaction
- Teachers left isolated in classrooms
- Professionally, emotionally or socially invasive leaders or colleagues
- Lack of affirmation and appreciation among staff and from leaders to staff and vice versa
- Judgmental attitudes between staff members and between leadership and staff
- Communication that is indirect, unclear and disrespectful
- Lack of safe forum to express need for help
- Ineffective discipline system
- Poor staff morale

❏ *Causes arising from school leadership*

A leader can make or break a school. Unless leaders are secure and confident, it is inevitable that they will project their vulnerabilities onto colleagues and students, be oversensitive to feedback and feel easily hurt, discouraged and unappreciated.

Effective leadership and discipline proceedings are seriously hampered when one or more of the following behaviours are manifested in the school leader:

- Finds challenges and risk-taking threatening
- Is non-inventive
- Has poor problem-solving skills
- Is addicted to work
- Hates job
- Dreads failure
- Is rigid in the face of difference
- Is intolerant of mistakes, failure and vulnerability
- Has unrealistic expectations of self, staff and students
- Is unavailable to staff or students
- Is unapproachable
- Is inattentive to needs of staff or students
- Is authoritarian or manipulative or passive in management style
- Is indecisive or unilateral in decision-making
- Does not consult with staff or students
- Does not affirm staff or students
- Is unable to appraise teachers' or students' efforts
- Shows poor conflict-resolution skills
- Undermines discipline system
- Is unpredictable and inconsistent
- Has poor or no management training
- Lacks ability to delegate responsibilities
- Does not respect confidentiality
- Displays nepotism
- Is unfriendly or hostile towards staff or students
- Is dismissive of teachers' or students' concerns
- Is overpleasing of parents to staff's detriment
- Does not listen to all sides

This list is not exhaustive; no doubt there are other causes of discipline problems that arise from the leadership of the school and it is up to teachers to document those causes and seek resolution of them.

❑ *Causes arising from school environment*

A school environment is emotional, social and physical in nature. An unfriendly emotional climate can prompt many disruptive or apathetic responses from leaders, teachers and students. A school that places pride only on academic performance can create a tense, anxious and strained atmosphere for all. Social and environmental causes of discipline problems include overcrowded conditions; large class size; undue pressure from parents, leaders and churches; and neglectful educational administration. Physical conditions can also lead to discipline problems: drab buildings and grounds; no playing or sports facilities; no display of teachers' or students' academic, sports and other non-academic achievements; inadequate ventilation or heating systems; small staffroom; few teaching resources; no sanction room; no parent room; lack of toilet facilities and relaxation areas.

❑ *Causes arising from outside home and school*

Discipline problems at home may be caused by persons or situations outside the home:

- Hostile neighbours can cause children to become fearful, timid and passive.
- Bullying in the neighbourhood can have marked effects on children's behaviours.
- Hidden emotional, physical or sexual abuse by someone outside the family can lead to emotional storms or withdrawal from reality.
- Peer-group pressure can lead to insecure children engaging in undisciplined conduct.
- Lack of appropriate recreational facilities provide a void that can be filled by delinquent activities.
- Lack of support structures for parents and children under stress means that problems go undetected and discipline problems continue to escalate.

- Interference from grandparents or other relations can cause confusion as to who really is in charge or resentment on the part of the young parent whose role is usurped.

Likewise at school, the causes of discipline problems may lie outside the school:

- A hostile neighbourhood can result in a school being vandalised.
- Students who have dropped out of school can be a threat to both school and community.
- High rates of unemployment can have marked effects on children's motivation to learn and attend school regularly.
- Bureaucratic government structures often lead to organisational neglect of teachers' and children's rights and needs.
- Teachers' unions that are more politically than people oriented have not been in the forefront of safeguarding teachers' rights.
- Undue influence of clergy in school management can lead to some teachers feeling judged and their philosophy of care for children undermined.

CHAPTER 4

Discipline Problems are Cries for Help

❑ *The protective nature of children's discipline problems*
❑ *The protective nature of parents' discipline problems*
❑ *The protective nature of teachers' discipline problems*
❑ *The cry for help in children's discipline problems*
❑ *The cry for help in parents' discipline problems*
❑ *The cry for help in teachers' discipline problems*
❑ *The unique nature of discipline problems*

❑ *The protective nature of children's discipline problems*

Children's under-controlled and over-controlled responses arise when their legitimate needs are not being met in homes, schools and communities. Like adults, children have a whole range of rights and needs that deserve to be listened to and fulfilled whenever possible. Examples of these needs are to be loved, to be affirmed and to be respected; a more detailed outline of children's rights and needs is given in Chapter 5. When any of these needs comes under threat, children will ingeniously develop ways to try to offset further threats. The experience of not having such essential needs met is devastating for children, and the more frequent, enduring and intense this neglect is, the greater the vulnerability of children and the stronger their need to protect against further slights to their expression of reasonable needs.

There are two main ways that children can protect against further hurt and loss: they can become either overdemanding or underdemanding. Both are ingenious responses to neglect. By being overdemanding, children may offset some rejection and get others to meet some of their needs, if only for 'peace sake'. In being underdemanding the underlying meaning for the child is 'if I never ask then I can't experience rejection'. Aggression is the main characteristic of overdemanding protective behaviour while passivity and avoidance are typical of underdemanding protective behaviour, avoidance and passivity being more common than aggression. Stereotyping has made it more likely that males will adopt the overdemanding protective strategy and females the underdemanding means of protection. The children who are seen to give most problems in homes, schools and communities are those who are aggressive and demanding. Nonetheless, the quiet, shy, reserved, timid and fearful children are also attempting to control adults into not hurting them and they need to be given as much attention as their aggressive peers.

The reason why the aggressive, uncooperative, loud, boastful and rebellious children are seen as the 'troublemakers' is that they make the lives of teachers and parents very difficult. This is not the intention of these children, but when teachers and parents think it is, they tend to lash out, thereby compounding the children's insecurity. The children, for instance, may be put out of class aggressively or may be 'put down' at home, but at least they have achieved their goal of getting the teacher or parent to back off from them.

An understanding of the protective nature of children's under-controlled or over-controlled behaviour is essential to the creation of an effective discipline system. This does not mean that parents and teachers have to sacrifice their rights and needs in the face of children's difficult actions; but it does mean that the assertion and safeguarding of rights and needs are done from a position of firmness, compassion and understanding.

❑ *The protective nature of parents' discipline problems*

Parents can employ over-controlled or under-controlled protective behaviours when faced with behaviours from their children or partners that threaten their basic needs of security. Many partners and parents come into these roles with long-term doubts about their lovability and capability and they have already developed a creative armentarium to protect themselves from further experiences of hurt and rejection.

Parents who are perfectionistic offset failure by taking great pains to get everything right. When their children fail, they view this as a threat to themselves ('people will think I'm a bad parent') and they may now rant and rave at the children to ensure that they do not fail again. The parents are not doing this to hurt the children, but to protect themselves from the judgment of others. Nevertheless, their vulnerability and protective strategies have a catastrophic effect on the children's emotional, intellectual and social development. These children learn at an early stage that 'it is not safe to fail'; that 'I must be clever and successful'; and that 'I must please others at all costs'. What a sad legacy these children inherit from their parents' insecurities and undisciplined responses.

There are parents who have learned to protect themselves by avoiding challenges, by going for the average, by apathy and passivity. When their children show drive and ambition, these parents will see these behaviours as threats to their protectors and, rather than encouraging such actions, they will bury them under a barrage of criticism, non-interest and dismissiveness. Once again, though never done deliberately, the lack of self-control on the part of these parents seriously blocks the development of their children.

Children have two alternatives in the face of parents' undisciplined and vulnerable behaviours: they can become like them ('if I'm like them they won't criticise me') or they can rebel ('if I control them they can't criticise me'). Either way, the children learn undesirable ways of getting their needs in life met. These children encounter many difficulties in schools, particularly those who take on their parents' pushy, perfectionistic or aggressive protectors or those who rebel against their parents' passivity.

Teachers know that the students who are persistent offenders come from troubled homes. It is important that teachers do not judge these parents as 'bad' or 'useless', but instead understand that their undesirable behaviours are mirrors of their vulnerability. Understanding, compassion and the non-directive offer of means of healing will go a long way to resolving both the parents' and the children's discipline problems.

❏ *The protective nature of teachers' discipline problems*

It is important to see that teachers, like students, employ protection and if, for example, a teacher feels slighted by a colleague or student she will find some way to reduce the possibility of a repeat experience of that hurt. The most common responses are:

- Passivity ('I'll say nothing so that I can't be slighted again')
- Avoidance ('if I stay out of his way I can't be put down again')
- Aggression ('I'll make sure she never does that to me again')
- Passive-aggression ('I'll make him pay in a way he'll never know')

All of these responses are undisciplined and show lack of self-control. These strategies or weapons against further hurt are intelligent, subtle, sophisticated and can sometimes be terrifying.

Many students (and their parents) complain of being 'put down' by teachers, not realising that these put downs are evidence of the emotional and social threats posed for the teachers by the students. This is not to say that students have to accept such undesirable behaviour, but when they see the vulnerability at its source they may be less likely to react with similar behaviour themselves. Certainly the students and their parents must assert their right to emotional, social, intellectual, physical and sexual safety in the classroom, but they need to do this in a way that is not judgmental and condemning of the teacher. Similarly, some students complain of teachers who are 'too soft', not realising that the passivity of these teachers is a wonderful protection against humiliation and hurt ('if I don't rock the boat, then I won't upset anybody'). Students are much more likely to be critical of teachers who use the protective weapons of cynicism and sarcasm than of those who use passivity as a protection, but it is important to realise that students also lose out in the development of security and self-control in the classes of passive teachers.

❏ *The cry for help in children's discipline problems*

There is another side to children's protective behaviours which is that they act to alert adults in the children's lives to hidden fears and insecurities; they are in effect cries for help. When direct expression of unmet needs is too emotionally risky for children, the wise part of their psyche finds ways to wake up adults to their failure to provide security and love. The greater the risk in directly expressing anger, sadness, fear and disappointment at not being loved and cared for, the louder will be the alerting message.

A twelve-year-old girl was sent to me for help because whatever the season every day she would throw herself fully clothed into a nearby river. She was also extremely hostile towards male teachers. In spite of verbal admonitions and sometimes physical beatings, she persisted in her daily ritual. Only when she found emotional safety in her therapeutic relationship did the truth emerge that her father was sexually abusing her and had threatened her life should she reveal the abuse. The river ritual and the troublesome behaviours at school were tickets into my practice and a means of warding off the threat of her father. By becoming a 'problem child' she ensured that people, in particular her mother, would keep a keen eye on her and, thereby, reduce the amount of time she was on her own with her father. It is vital that parents and teachers look for the alerting message in the ill-disciplined behaviours of children. It is the healing of the hidden hurts and vulnerabilities which the protective behaviours are signalling that leads to the ultimate resolution of discipline problems.

A fifteen-year-old student was referred to me because he had a tendency to 'give cheek' to teachers. He also avoided doing homework assignments and did his utmost to disrupt classes. No teachers or students should have to tolerate such blocking of their legitimate needs for order, respect and attention to learning. The resolution does not lie in berating the student, but it does require that he be removed from the classroom until the hidden reasons for his protective and disruptive actions are resolved. When I met the boy's father I found him to be highly aggressive and critical towards the boy. The boy told me that he felt he could never please or be good enough for his father, so why should he bother? Rather than succumbing to his father's domination of him, he rebelled and in doing so took on the very characteristics he hated in his father. When any teacher attempted to control him in ways similar to his father, he reacted aggressively. Teachers who treated him kindly and fairly had no discipline problems with him. The boy's 'cry for help' was to be treated by his father and teachers in loving, accepting, valuing, and fair and firm ways. He did not want to experience being ridiculed. His father was very responsive to his son's needs and recognised that he himself had been treated in the same critical way by his own father. A closer relationship developed between them and the boy's difficulties in school decreased significantly. Part of the boy's healing was to learn to confront teachers who were not respectful in ways that were not retaliatory but assertive.

❑ *The cry for help in parents' discipline problems*

Parents are the family architects and their daily ways of responding to children are the greatest determinants of their children's level of security and self-esteem. Examples of the under-controlled responses of parents that adversely affect children are threatening to leave, withdrawal of love, irritability, constant criticism and physical punishment. Parents do not intend these undesirable responses to block their children's development, but that is their effect. These ill-disciplined reactions are protective attempts to 'whip children into shape' so that they cannot become a threat to the parents' security. However, as long as parents do not heed the alerting message of their damaging actions, they themselves will remain vulnerable and their children's security will continue to be threatened.

Many parents come for help because they cannot accept certain behaviours in their children, most notably academic failure. This lack of tolerance is a clear message to them about their own fears of failure and their need to resolve this vulnerability for the sake of themselves and their children.

Some parents (more often than not male) punish severely any display of crying in a child, particularly a son. I recall one case where a mother kept beating her two-year-old son until he stopped crying. Fifty years later he had not cried again. These parents need to perceive that crying is an act of strength and that weakness lies in hiding the emotion.

It must be seen too that parents' over-controlled responses to children are alerting messages about the parents themselves and, unless corrected, will have lasting and serious effects on children's development. Examples of the over-controlled responses of parents include:

- Absence of love and affection
- Overprotection
- Lack of encouragement
- Not standing up for children
- Doing everything for children
- Giving too much responsibility to children
- Spoiling children
- Few or no expectations of children
- Not allowing children to have friends in home
- Keeping children tied to home
- Fussing over children
- Not trusting children to do things for themselves

❑ *The cry for help in teachers' discipline problems*

Just as with children and parents, the ill-disciplined behaviours of teachers signal the need for healing and change. When a teacher is irritable in the classroom there is a clear message that some need is not being met in the relationship with the students and that their behaviour is a threat to the emotional and social security of the teacher. It may be, for example, that the irritation arises because the students are not measuring up to the teacher's standards for academic performance. The students' failure to live up to standards is a threat to the teacher's vulnerable self-image. In her under-controlled reaction the teacher confuses the students' poor academic performance with her own need for success, and the resulting irritability is a subconscious attempt to get the students to toe the teacher's line. The teacher needs to see that her irritability is alerting her to her vulnerability and the need to take responsibility to heal her own dependence on success and other people's opinions of her.

When I think back on my own experiences as a primary and secondary teacher, I cringe at many of my under-controlled responses to students – and I was regarded as being a 'nice' teacher! I have many regrets and I do feel responsible for any hurts I inflicted, but I do not feel guilty. I was deeply vulnerable at that stage of my life and my overreactions to students were messages to me to get help for my many unresolved hurts. This way of interpreting my behaviour does not justify my unacceptable responses to students but it does explain them and allows for the possibility of change through healing. The pity is that at that time I was not ready for change and there was no supportive milieu for change in the school setting (the opposite in fact was the case).

In recent years I have worked with a number of teachers referred to me for violence towards pupils. These teachers did not set out to hurt students but they had a terror of not being seen to be in charge of their classrooms. Aggression was a means of ensuring no display of under-controlled behaviour from their students. The aggressive responses were alerting these teachers to their own insecurities and the need to take responsibility for resolving them rather than projecting them onto students.

The powerful weapons of cynicism, sarcasm, ostracisation, dismissiveness and ridicule can be even greater threats than physical violence to the emotional, social and intellectual well-being of students. It is vital that teachers who engage in such protective reactions take the message from them that it is they, not the students, who need the greater help.

❑ *The unique nature of discipline problems*

The same difficult behaviour in two or more children will have very different functions and its alerting message will also be different for different children. Each child's behaviour is peculiar to that child and it is not wise to generalise; the same holds true for adults. Each child has his own ingenious reasons for expressing his insecurities in undisciplined ways. However, it can certainly be broadly assumed that aggressive or passive behaviours spring from a need to be loved and valued and are preceded by some experience wherein the child felt hurt, angered, rejected, humiliated or 'put down'. The constructive approach is to provide the child with warmth and security and to determine what hurt, angered or upset him. Such a response is often an eye-opener for parents and alerts them to the need on their part for change towards the child; it also provides an opportunity for both parties to learn from the upsetting experience.

A student who had been suspended from school because of verbal aggression towards a teacher revealed to me that this under-controlled behaviour occurred only with certain teachers. Teachers who treated her with respect and were fair and just found reciprocal responses from her. However, those who employed protective behaviours of sarcasm and public ridicule experienced similar responses from her. Her suspension further enraged her, as it appeared there was one rule for teachers and another for students whereby it was permissible for a teacher to 'put down' a student but not vice versa. Her immediate response to the sarcasm of a teacher was to hurtle abuse at her. This response was intended subconsciously to control the teacher into not again treating the student in this fashion. However, there was a deeper issue, which was that the critical behaviour of the teacher reminded her of her parents' typical treatment of her; the anger and rage she felt towards them but dare not vent, she displaced onto the teacher. Both the student and the teacher had much to learn from their reactions to each other:

- Both of them were employing aggression as a protector against further hurt and humiliation
- The home situation of the student was contributing to her reactions to a particular teacher
- A double standard of behaviour was operating

- There was a need for mutual respect and caring between teacher and student
- The student's relationship with her parents needed exploration and resolution
- Both student and teacher needed to apologise for their ill-disciplined responses to each other.

The involvement of this girl's parents was central to the resolution of her discipline problems.

PART III

Discipline is about Safeguarding Rights

CHAPTER 5

The Rights of Children, Parents and Teachers

❑ *What safeguarding rights means*
❑ *Rights common to all*
  - The right to physical safety
  - The right to sexual safety
  - The right to emotional safety
  - The right to intellectual safety
  - The right to social safety
  - The right to creative safety

❑ *Children's rights within the home*
❑ *Students' rights within the school*
  - The right to be addressed by preferred title
  - The right to learn in a positive atmosphere
  - The right to fail and the right to succeed
  - The right to fair, just and effective teaching
  - The right to request help when experiencing personal, interpersonal or educational difficulties

❑ *Parents' rights*
❑ *Teachers' rights*
  - The right to physical, emotional, social, intellectual, creative and sexual safety
  - The right to respect
  - The right to teach in an atmosphere of order and attention
  - The right to be communicated with in direct and clear ways
  - The right to demand social structures within the school that guarantee respect for rights
  - The right to ask for help when needed
  - The right to fair, just and effective leadership
  - The right to express needs and grievances
  - The right to have recourse to social structures that protect rights

❏ *What safeguarding rights means*

Recently there have been a number of tragic murders in Ireland of women who had managed to obtain legal protection orders against their violent husbands but who, nevertheless, were murdered by them. The state failed miserably in safeguarding the rights of these women to live in safety without threats of invasion of their homes, their persons and their lives. An increasing phenomenon is that both parents and teachers are experiencing verbal and physical attacks by children, and some have been murdered. Of course, it is not a new phenomenon that children are also subjected to such acts of aggression by parents and teachers. An even more worrying development is children bullying and even murdering peers. Structures are needed to ensure that the legitimate rights of all the members of a community are not jeopardised as they are in these examples, but instead are upheld and safeguarded.

Safeguarding structures must have two dimensions: the first dimension is a focus on the individual who is at risk from a person showing under-controlled behaviours and the second dimension involves a focus on the perpetrator. It would seem in the case of the women who were murdered by their violent partners that there was a serious deficit in the structures that would ensure that these men, having been shown to be violent, would never again darken the door of their partners' homes. Serious consideration must be given to the development of monitoring procedures which ensure that violent individuals obey the requirements of a protection order. Words rarely control the behaviour of people who resort to violence; actions are far more likely to achieve this objective. Clearly, the frequency, intensity and duration of the violent responses are a barometer of the level of active safeguarding systems that will be required to ensure safety for the victims of violence. Similarly, children, parents, teachers and people in authority require social structures that they can call on when they are at risk from under-controlled behaviours. The earlier the message goes out from individuals themselves and from back-up social structures that no disrespect of an oral, written or physical nature will be tolerated in homes, schools and communities, the less the likelihood of gross under-controlled actions.

Generally speaking, it is poorer people who have not been educated to declare and safeguard their legitimate rights, including the right to back-up community supports. Whilst there has been some development in social concern for children and women who have been victims of physical or sexual abuse, there has been little development in safeguarding the right to physical safety of parents and teachers. And what have not been considered at all are the equally important rights of children and adults to emotional, intellectual and social safety.

Unless the two-pronged safeguarding actions suggested above are taken in relation to the emotional, physical, sexual, intellectual and social rights of both children and adults in homes, schools and communities, far more serious discipline problems will emerge within these social systems. However, as long as discipline is seen as being there only for the perpetrators of undisciplined conduct, then the victims will continue to be at risk and the perpetrators will only be reinforced in their undesirable ways of behaving. The whole purpose of discipline procedures must be to safeguard the rights of victims and to help those people who resort to ill-disciplined behaviours to find more appropriate and effective ways of getting their unmet needs met. It is wise to remember that persons who engage in undisciplined actions have the same rights as their victims to physical, sexual, emotional, intellectual and social safety. Ill-disciplined behaviour cannot be countered with similar protective reactions; to do so simply serves to escalate matters, and both parties to the conflict wind up even more hurt and rejected. When one party can hold on to his own self-respect, spell out clearly his rights and, when necessary, resort to the back-up resources that value and respond actively to his stance, then a happier outcome can be predicted.

There are several important aspects to the development of a discipline system that is focused on safeguarding rights:

- An awareness and acceptance of the legitimate rights of children, parents and teachers (below)
- The development of the concept of mutual responsibility (Chapter 6)
- The creation of means to empower children and adults to stand up for their rights (Chapter 7)

- The development of social structures in homes, schools and communities that value and safeguard the rights of children and adults (Chapters 8, 9 and 10)
- The recognition that the self-discipline of adults is paramount in any system of discipline (Chapter 11)
- The acceptance that prevention needs to be a central part of a discipline system (Chapter 12)
- The understanding that the resolution of discipline problems is a collective responsibility (Chapter 13)

❑ *Rights common to all*

One of the most vital aspects in the vindication of the rights of people is that 'right' does not mean 'might'. On the contrary, you are responsible for your own rights. When you make other people responsible for your rights, you are likely to blame and condemn them when your rights are not met. Such a reaction will only send you into the unhappy spiral of either judging, blaming, condemning and forcing others or self-blaming and passivity. Either way, your legitimate needs will go unfulfilled, as will the rights of those you attack or from whom you withdraw. Children need adults to safeguard their rights, but the sooner they are helped to be aware of and own their rights themselves, the better for them and all others.

An important distinction must be made between rights and needs. Whilst every right is a need, not every need is a right. For example, a teacher's need to be respected by students and colleagues is clearly a legitimate right. However, a teacher may have a need to be consulted on certain decisions made by the school principal but would not be deemed to have the right to such consultation. Of course, the school principal who ignores that need is unlikely to get cooperation and support from the teacher involved. The distinction between rights and needs is reflected also, for instance, in children's right to be loved by their parents as against their need to exercise choice in what they eat. Whilst children's right to be loved would be seen as legitimate, it is unlikely that many parents are in a position to meet their need to choose what they may eat. Nevertheless, some acceptance of children's food likes and dislikes may offset some of the conflict that can arise at mealtimes. In considering ways of responding to discipline problems, it is best to stick to the clear-cut rights of teachers, children and parents.

A distinction too is required between reasonable needs and unreasonable or unrealistic ones. It certainly is reasonable for a teacher to expect to be consulted by her principal on matters that affect her work, but to demand to be consulted on every minor decision would be unreasonable. Similarly, a teacher may have a reasonable expectation that students complete assigned homework, but to expect students to do work during school holidays would be unreasonable. Many discipline problems arise because of unreasonable demands on the part of parents, teachers and principals.

The rights of both children and adults revolve primarily around six dimensions of human life:

- Physical
- Sexual
- Emotional
- Intellectual
- Social
- Creative

People have the right to feel safe in all areas of life and any threat to safety must be responded to with firm, consistent and predictable actions on the part of victims or guardians of victims.

■ The right to physical safety

Threats to the right to physical safety can take many forms: pushing, spitting, slapping, verbally threatening ('we'll get you'), force-feeding, bullying, physically intimidating, threatening with weapons and sarcastic comments on physical appearance.

■ The right to sexual safety

Recent years have revealed that the sexual integrity of children has suffered innumerable violations in all the social systems in which children participate (homes, schools, churches, sports clubs, neighbourhoods). The boundaries of adults too, particularly women, have experienced and continue to experience considerable abuse. Everyone deserves and has an inalienable right to sexual safety. Violations of this right of children by adults or peers can involve:

- Inappropriate touching and holding
- Sexualising children before their time
- Exposing children to sexual materials (magazines, videos)
- Talking explicitly on sexual matters
- Sexually exposing self
- Getting children to touch an adult's or peer's erogenous zones
- Attempting or accomplishing vaginal, anal or oral intercourse

■ The right to emotional safety

The right to emotional safety is basic to safeguarding the emotional life of the adult and child. Feelings are the most accurate and wisest barometer of what is happening to a person at any one moment of time. Unfortunately, emotions are seen by many people as threatening, and responses of dismissal, suppression, repression, dilution or projection are more common than honest and open emotional expression and responsivity. Many children have been prevented by parents and teachers from the expression of fear, hurt, sadness, loneliness, depression, despair, anger and outrage. The inner world of these children remains hidden and this emotional underworld can be often the covert source for discipline problems. Examples of threats to emotional integrity are:

- Laughing at or mocking a person's fears
- Dismissing feelings ('don't tell me about it'; 'not now, maybe later')
- Diluting feelings ('it's not as bad as you feel it is'; 'you'll feel better about it tomorrow')
- Suppressing feelings ('you shouldn't be upset'; 'don't be angry')
- Punishing feelings ('stop that crying'; 'you make me so angry when you're fearful')

- Neutralising feelings, by showing no recognition of the feeling ('you'll feel differently tomorrow'; 'so what, we all feel that at times')

■ The right to intellectual safety

The right to intellectual safety is frequently violated by many people, both young and old, who experience considerable ridiculing of their own intellectual ability. Most people confuse knowledge with intelligence, and knowledge is often used as a means of feeling superior and making others feel inferior. But knowledge is an index of learning, not a measure of intelligence. Intelligence is our vast and unlimited potential to adapt to and understand the world we live in. The right to intellectual safety involves acknowledgment of this given and an acceptance of the person's present ways of making sense and order out of his world. Threats to intellectual safety for both children and adults can come in many ways:

- Labelling ('you're stupid'; 'you're a fool'; 'you're slow'; 'you're weak')
- Dismissing opinions ('what would you know about anything?'; 'what you're saying is stupid')
- Criticising perceptions and ways of doing things ('how could you possibly see it that way?'; 'there is no other way to do this')
- Ridiculing efforts to learn ('you call that making an effort?'; 'you better learn to "pull up your socks" young man')
- Making comparisons ('class B would let you lot in the shade'; 'there is no way you'll be as bright as your sister')
- Using sarcasm in response to learning efforts ('who was the fool who wrote this?'; 'a monkey could do better')
- Being impatient and irritable with learning efforts ('come on, get on with it')
- Making it emotionally unsafe to fail ('this class does not tolerate failure'; 'let me read out this stupid answer')
- Putting pressure on to succeed ('I expect you all to get As in this subject'; 'last year's class did remarkably well')

■ The right to social safety

The social presence of every human being is a unique phenomenon and each person has the right to acknowledgment of
that specialness. We violate other people's right to social safety
when we:

- Ignore their presence or absence
- Do not address them by their preferred title
- Turn away from them
- Leave them isolated
- Ostracise them
- Make snide comments about them
- Show non-verbal hostility to their presence ('looking down
  one's nose'; hostile facial expression)
- Do not include them in conversation
- Are not hospitable towards them
- Openly express hostility towards them
- Make sarcastic comments ('what are you doing here?' or 'I
  certainly didn't expect you to turn up here')

There is no greater boost to either children or adults than to
let them know warmly and genuinely, 'you are one of a kind
and special'.

■ The right to creative safety

The greatest needs of the human psyche are to be loved and
to be free to live out its own unique existence. Being loved is
the passport that allows us the freedom to be ourselves.

Pressure to conform is the strongest block preventing people
from exercising their right to live out their lives in their own
unique and creative way. Forcing children into behaviours that
are not right for them is also a gross infringement of this
right. Intolerance of differences in opinions and beliefs is yet
another violation. The irony is that when people are allowed
the freedom to be themselves and to explore the world in their
own unique and creative ways, they are far more productive
and self-fulfilled and, as a consequence, society benefits greatly.

The source of many discipline problems is that too many students, parents and teachers are pushed into living against the grain of their own unique being.

❏ *Children's rights within the home*

The era of children having second-class citizenship within the home is gone and children are now much more aware that, like adults, they also have rights. It is the responsibility of all adults to help children to be aware of their rights. Sometimes the last place where children are introduced to their rights is in the home. The school, church and community can do much to redress such a lack. No longer can people turn a blind eye to the rights of children under the banner 'it is up to the parents'.

Children's rights within the home	
• I have the right to physical, emotional, social, intellectual, creative and sexual safety. • I have the right to unconditional love. • I have the right to accept-ance of my unique self. • I have the right to care and nurturance. • I have the right to fair, just and effective parenting.	• I have the right to be communicated with in direct and clear ways. • I have the right to fail and the right to succeed. • I have the right to be educated. • When rights are being violated, I have the right to seek help outside the home.

Unconditional love is the deepest longing and most funda-mental right of all children. It is the *sine qua non* for the overall well-being of children. Children also need to be accepted for their unique selves and not forced into conformity with the projections of parents, teachers and others. Furthermore, children have the right to be cared for and nurtured and the right to fair, just and effective parenting. When parents are inconsistent in responding to their children's rights or are unable to uphold them, it is incumbent on other adults to assert these children's rights. Children's right to be educated can be thwarted by parents' own bad experiences of schooling or their own inferiority feelings about education. No matter what the sources of disruption, schools and school attendance officers must see to it that children are not deprived of appropriate educational opportunities. Visible sources of help need to be made available for children whose rights are under threat in the home.

❑ *Students' rights within the school*

There is not a lot of difference between the rights of teachers and students. Equalising the relationship between teachers and students is one of the bases for effective discipline. Teachers, however, have a position of authority which means that they carry greater responsibilities than others in the school system and need structures that support the execution of these responsibilities.

Students need to be made aware of their rights and empowered to act on them. Like teachers, students should not have to put up with even the slightest disrespect of their rights. Unless teachers own the fact that they frequently do violate the rights of students, little progress can be made on the discipline issue.

Students' rights within the school

- I have the right to be respected by teachers and peers.
- I have the right to be addressed by my preferred title.
- I have the right to learn in a positive atmosphere.
- I have the right to fail and the right to succeed.
- I have the right to fair, just and effective teaching.
- I have the right to be communicated with in direct and clear ways.
- I have the right to physical, emotional, social, intellectual, creative and sexual safety.

- I have the right to demand social structures that safeguard my rights.
- When my rights are threatened by teachers or peers, I have the right to ask for help.
- I have the right to request help when experiencing personal, interpersonal or educational difficulties.
- When teachers or peers are not responsive to expressed grievances, I have the right to go to others in authority for help.

As mentioned, students and teachers share many of the same rights and these rights are discussed below under the heading of teachers' rights. Five of the students' rights listed above are particular to them and so are elaborated on here:

- I have the right to be addressed by my preferred title.
- I have the right to learn in a positive atmosphere.
- I have the right to fail and the right to succeed.
- I have the right to fair, just and effective teaching.
- I have the right to request help when experiencing personal, interpersonal or educational difficulties.

■ The right to be addressed by preferred title

Calling the student by his preferred title (which generally is the student's first name) is an act of respect and serves to raise self-esteem. It is not acceptable that teachers call students by names other than their preferred titles and do not make genuine efforts to recall the names of students.

■ The right to learn in a positive atmosphere

Students have a right to be taught by teachers in ways that do not undermine their sense of self and self-confidence. The school system can no longer allow the vulnerabilities of teachers and limited professional training to be excuses for unacceptable teaching interactions with students. Provision needs to be made to reduce both the personal and professional deficits of teachers. When the source of conflict within the classroom is other students' ill-disciplined conduct, the school system must not allow the rights of the 'in-control' students to be blocked.

■ The right to fail and the right to succeed

In my profession as a clinical psychologist I help as many people who are fearful of success as those who are fearful of failure. The fear of failure is not a surprise to most people as there are few of us who do not dread mistakes and getting things wrong. Although less well recognised, the fear of success is just as debilitating and leads many students to aim for average results rather than aiming towards maximising their resources. 'Going for the average' is a marvellous protection as it reduces parents' and teachers' expectations. To attain success means then having to maintain it and facing the risk of rejection should the student fall from his pedestal.

Failure and success are relative terms; there is nobody who does not have a mixture of both experiences on a daily basis. The labelling of any child as a 'failure' must stop as it can have profound effects on self-esteem. Furthermore, failure and success are integral to learning; failure is the riser in the step of learning and success is the tread. The old saying 'the man who never made a mistake, never made anything' sums up well this philosophy.

Teachers do their profession a disservice by being critical of failure and overpraising of success. It is not wise to use these essential aspects of learning as means of motivating students. The danger is that students either come to hate and avoid learning or attempt to prove themselves through learning. Either way, learning becomes a fearful experience and children's natural curiosity and eagerness to learn dry up under these threats to their self-esteem.

Children have the right to fail and the right to succeed: teachers serve students well by respecting these rights and placing their focus on and encouraging efforts to learn.

■ The right to fair, just and effective teaching

There are excellent teachers in the educational system but there are also those who are not effective and do not inspire children with a love of and a sound grounding in knowledge. This is not a condemnation of the teachers, but of the educational system which long ago should have detected these teachers and either helped them to become more effective or arranged, without loss of face, for transfer to another, more appropriate area of public service. Children's education will influence the rest of their lives and no stone should be left unturned to ensure effective teaching of students.

■ The right to request help when experiencing personal, interpersonal or educational difficulties

When many of us were children there was no forum for the expression of the turmoil experienced in the school or classroom. Parents tended to be in awe of teachers, and children feared that if they complained they would risk being blamed themselves for their dissatisfactions in school. Children have every right to express any problems they experience in school and it is crucial that teachers, parents and significant others listen and, when appropriate, act on students' complaints.

❑ *Parents' rights*

Even though parents perform the most valuable role in society, they are the most neglected in terms of preparation and continued support for that role, and also in terms of awareness and maintenance of their own rights. When their rights are neglected, the consequences can be serious not only for the parents but also for children and teachers. Where there are two parents, the rights of the partner also have to be considered and failure to uphold these rights equally can have devastating effects on the family and school. Parents also have rights in relation to school and poor liaison between home and school can create many difficulties for parents, teachers and students. But what is most ignored is that parents have rights in relation to their children.

While it is important for parents to be aware of and to respond positively to their children's needs, it is equally important that they are aware of their own rights in their relationships with their children and the teachers of their children. There are many parents who do not give any time, consideration or resources to upholding their own rights and instead put an overemphasis on being there for their children. Neither do these parents assert their rights to be involved in and consulted on their children's education. Such passivity on the part of parents means that they do not model for their children the necessity of knowing and standing up for their own rights and the rights of others. There are other parents whose rights are continually besieged by the under-controlled behaviour of their children and by teachers who are dismissive of their involvement in their children's education.

Parents' rights	
• I have the right to physical, emotional, social, intellectual, creative and sexual safety in the home, school and community. • I have the right to be loved and respected by my partner and children. • I have the right to ask for fair sharing of child rearing by my partner. • I have the right to be communicated with in direct and clear ways by my partner, my children and their teachers.	• I have the right to personal independence. • I have the right to financial equality and security. • I have the right to be involved in and consulted on my children's education. • When concerned about my child's educational progress, I have the right to approach the school. • When any of my rights are violated, I have the right to seek help and support services outside the home.

Parents need as much help as possible to safeguard their rights in the performance of such an important role. The benefit of such support will stretch beyond the home into schools and also into communities, churches and workplaces.

❑ *Teachers' rights*

The cry for help on how to cope with the rising tide of discipline problems is loudest from teachers. Teaching is one of the most neglected professions in terms of failure to uphold the rights of teachers to physical, social and emotional safety and, indeed, in the case of female teachers, sexual safety. Unacceptable breaches of the rights of teachers are now being perpetrated and these demand to be remedied immediately.

The evidence that the rights and needs of teachers are not enshrined in the social structure in which they are employed is that teaching has become the second most stressful occupation after mining. High absenteeism among teachers is due primarily to stress, anxiety and back pain (which is the most frequently occurring symptom of stress). Many teachers now claim to hate teaching. The drop-out rate from teaching is high and it is certainly no longer seen as a desirable and challenging profession. It is a sorry indication of the system's neglect of teachers that they are now more at risk than even police officers and prison officers and under greater stress than medical doctors and social workers.

As long as teachers wait for others to uphold their rights, they are powerless and will continue to be victims of outrageous misfortune. However, when they respect and own their own rights and show determination to create and use structures to maintain those rights, then teaching may become the rewarding profession that it can be.

Teachers' rights
<ul><li>I have the right to physical, emotional, social, intellectual, creative and sexual safety.</li><li>I have the right to respect from students, colleagues, leaders and parents.</li><li>I have the right to teach in an atmosphere of order and attention.</li><li>I have the right to be communicated with in direct and clear ways.</li><li>I have the right to demand social structures within the school that guarantee respect for my rights.</li></ul>	<ul><li>I have the right to ask for help when needed.</li><li>I have the right to fair, just and effective leadership on the part of the school principal and vice-principal.</li><li>I have the right to express any need or grievance I may have.</li><li>When any of my rights are violated, I have the right to have recourse to social structures within and outside the school that protect those rights.</li></ul>

These rights may seem self-evident and to demand no elucidation, but unfortunately there is evidence to suggest that they are not upheld in many schools.

■ The right to physical, emotional, social, intellectual, creative and sexual safety

This right implies that no teacher should have to tolerate any physical aggression, sexual harassment, public humiliation, sarcasm, shouting, disruption or lack of cooperation from students, colleagues, management or parents. Many teachers feel that this fundamental right is under constant threat in both the classroom and the staffroom, but it is up to them to value strongly this right and find ways to uphold it.

■ The right to respect

Mutual respect, whether between teacher and student, teacher and teacher, teacher and leader or teacher and parent, is the hallmark of a supportive, enriching and dynamic relationship. Every human being is worthy of respect. It is the violation of this most basic of rights that underlies many discipline problems. A prime need of all human beings is to be loved, valued, cherished, recognised for self and respected, and teachers carry this need into the classroom, staffroom, school and community. When the teacher herself does not prioritise this need, she puts herself at great emotional and social risk. When the school does not enshrine this primary need within its mission statement and school policies, it puts its teachers at great risk. Likewise, if government educational policy does not endorse this need, the country will have a workforce with low morale, low self-esteem and high stress levels.

The popular notion that people must earn respect from another contradicts the inherent right to respect from others. The former belief is conditional in nature and implies that it is through your actions that you earn respect. This is a recipe for discipline problems because people are not their behaviour. When you show respect to another you are honouring that person's unique being. There may be behaviours that threaten, disgust or alienate you, but these need to be handled in a respectful manner. To do otherwise would be to engage in the very behaviours you are condemning.

- The right to teach in an atmosphere of order and attention

Teachers get trained to teach and they have a right to pursue that professional goal without undue hindrance. No teacher should have to spend time trying to control a class. There is something radically wrong with the school system when this happens. Even when the teacher may be the main cause of the undisciplined behaviour of students, it is still the system that needs correction. Two questions have to be asked when this is the case: one, why did the students not use a legitimate structure to complain about their unmet needs within the classroom and, two, why did the structures not show up the ill-disciplined behaviours on the part of the teacher?

- The right to be communicated with in direct and clear ways

When others (students, colleagues, parents, management) have needs of a teacher, these must be communicated in a way that is direct and clear. 'Direct' means that the message is addressed to the person for whom it is intended, and 'clear' means that an 'I' message about a specific need is what is communicated. For example, 'Sir, I would like you to address me by my first name' is a direct and clear communication. Typically, people communicate with 'you' messages; for example, 'Miss, you should call me by my first name.' The problem with the 'you' message is that the student is not owning his own need to be addressed by his first name, and, secondly, he is attempting to control the teacher into meeting his need – 'you should . . .' The teacher cannot afford to respond to this type of communication as it would jeopardise her right to direct and clear communication. The student is entitled to make a request but not to order the teacher to meet his need. In order to keep her right intact, the teacher would do well to help the student to see the difference between requesting and ordering and to indicate her willingness to respond to the former but not to the latter.

- The right to demand social structures within the school that guarantee respect for rights

Teachers have a right to demand from the Department of Education structures within the school that guarantee that their rights are safeguarded. When such structures do not exist, teachers must create them themselves and continue to demand ratification of them by the Department of Education. Of course, these safeguarding structures for teachers' rights must not threaten the rights of others. If managers and school principals resist the implementation of safeguarding structures, teachers must continue to pursue them until they find the safety that they deserve.

Once a secondary school teacher who was being heckled and called names in the classroom approached me for help. On analysis it was clear that the teacher was not doing anything to precipitate such undesirable responses and it was clear also that the school, and particularly the principal, had tolerated the under-controlled behaviours of this group of students and was unwilling to impose sanctions on them. The principal showed no consideration for the teacher's plight and rationalised that these students came from difficult homes and the school should do everything to keep them in the school. But at what expense! The teacher now hated teaching, was under major stress, had developed high blood-pressure and felt like 'throwing in the towel'. Neither were the students being helped. Their disruptive behaviours not only blocked the teacher's rights to teach and to be respected but also blocked the right to learn on the part of the other students and themselves. Where then was the principal's caring for the perpetrators of the undisciplined behaviour? Two responses were needed in this situation: firstly, to uphold the rights of the class teacher and the other students, and secondly, to attempt to resolve the causes behind the disruptive behaviours of the perpetrators. However, the latter response must not be allowed to take precedence over the former, as it was in the situation described here.

I suggested to the teacher that he approach the principal and ask for assistance on the matter. He did so but got little response. I then advised him to return to the principal and state that he was unwilling to continue to take this class unless actions were taken to resolve the untenable situation. This time there were promises, but no action. The final sanction for the teacher was to inform the principal that unless the four students involved were removed from the class he would not take the class. He followed through on this sanction. Only then did the principal remove the students from the class and set up a consultative committee to help them. Within a month the students requested to be allowed to return to the teacher's class. No further disruption occurred.

■ The right to ask for help when needed

Weakness is strength. In requesting help there is openness about vulnerability and it is through this acceptance that there are opportunities to learn how to cope more effectively. Many teachers are frightened of expressing experiences of having difficult classes or unfair treatment by colleagues or principals because of their fear of being judged or criticised.

■ The right to fair, just and effective leadership

The level of personal security of the school principal and her attitudes towards staff and students can have a profound effect on individual teachers and on overall staff morale. Personal effectiveness is the foundation of professional effectiveness. When leaders lack personal effectiveness they are likely to be aggressive, dogmatic, rigid and inflexible or passive, overpleasing, indecisive and conflict-avoiders or manipulative, sarcastic and defensive. Many teachers complain that principals do not listen to or value or take action on their basic rights to emotional, social and physical safety. These teachers speak of the lack of staff meetings, poor or overrigid discipline systems and hostility to any attempts at change. Some teachers experience outright abuse from principals.

Clearly, this is not acceptable and teachers themselves must come together to counter such ineffective leadership where it occurs. They need to assert strongly their right to fair, just and effective leadership and take firm action when such leadership is not forthcoming. Actions could include, for example, taking their own initiative on issues, or writing a policy document and submitting this to all concerned – staff, principal, vice-principal, parents' association, board of management and school inspectorate. Sometimes the radical action of 'downing tools' may be required to bring about more effective leadership. Such confrontation is an act of caring, not only for the teachers but also for the principal. To ignore neglect is a rejection of self, and collusion with a leader's vulnerability only serves to perpetuate her problems. Confrontation, on the other hand, means that opportunities for growth are available for all.

The Department of Education must also have some formal means of evaluating the effectiveness of leaders, as much for the department's sake as for the sake of school staffs and students.

■ The right to express needs and grievances

When the grievances of teachers are not expressed they become like a hidden cancer that eats into the school's effectiveness. Teachers then can become hostile, resentful, apathetic and clock-watching. If a teacher has personal difficulty in voicing grievances she needs to explore how she can support herself and resolve this difficulty, at least to the extent that she will no longer tolerate neglect of her rights. It is an act of undisciplined behaviour not to act on unmet rights. Identifying and proactively responding to the causes of passivity is vital. Sometimes the causes may lie within interpersonal relationships where it is not safe to express grievances. The teacher may have learnt that to say nothing means eliminating the risk of humiliation, sarcasm, dismissiveness and judgment. In such a situation the teacher may need the help of an informal support group to lend back-up to her expression of difficulties.

■ The right to have recourse to social structures that protect rights

The creation of structures that protect and support the rights of teachers has not been high on the agenda of schools. But unless these structures are developed there will be a continuity in the exodus from the ranks of the teaching profession and it will be seen as an undesirable career. It is important that when structures do exist teachers use their right to employ them to protect all of their rights.

CHAPTER 6

Mutual Responsibility

❑ *Rights and responsibilities go hand in hand*
❑ *Parents' responsibilities towards children*
❑ *Children's responsibilities towards parents*
❑ *Children's responsibilities towards each other*
❑ *Students' responsibilities towards teachers*
❑ *Teachers' responsibilities towards students*
❑ *Teachers' responsibilities towards each other*
❑ *Teachers' responsibilities towards principals*
❑ *Principals' responsibilities towards teachers*
❑ *Teachers' responsibilities towards parents*
❑ *Parents' responsibilities towards teachers*

❑ *Rights and responsibilities go hand in hand*

The statement of rights on its own ensures nothing. Rights only have meaning when they are seen within relationships. Relationships are the primary medium through which people get their needs met in all social systems. When people's needs are met few discipline problems arise. Accordingly, where there is mutual respect and determination to meet each other's needs between parents and children then rights have meaning. The same holds true for the relationship in the school between teacher and student, teacher and teacher, principal and teacher, and teacher and parents. This also applies to people and their community.

It follows from this that mutual responsibility is basic to the vindication of rights. For example, teachers need to make clear requests of those in the school system and others associated with it. These requests for actions that ensure teachers' rights become the responsibilities that students, colleagues, managers and parents have towards teachers. Teachers must not forget that responsibility is a two-way process: students, colleagues, managers and parents have similar rights and the need for consequent actions on the part of teachers. The lack of recognition of and inaction on this two-way responsibility is a significant cause of the discipline problems that can occur in schools and homes. Teachers and parents can operate double standards, and children are quick to recognise the injustice of this and are far less inclined to respond to the rights and needs of their parents and teachers. Children, like adults, respond well to fairness and justice.

❏ *Parents' responsibilities towards children*

The failure of parents to uphold their children's rights and meet their legitimate needs is a major cause of discipline problems within homes, schools and communities. Children respond to the dynamics of the family, and so when the interactions are of a conditional and depriving nature, children react with either over-controlled or under-controlled behaviours. Parents do not deliberately harm their children, but they cannot give to their children the maturity they do not possess themselves. Parents bring their emotional baggage into their homes and, subconsciously, load their children with similar vulnerability. Parents need all the help they can get, but instead have been really neglected in the preparation for and the

Parents' responsibilities towards children	
• Demonstrate unconditional love • Accept their uniqueness • Meet reasonable physical, emotional, social, intellectual, educational, behavioural and creative needs • Listen to them • Spend undistracted time with them • Be patient with them • Apologise when undisciplined	• Play with them • Do not impose own needs on them • Try to discover the unique ways they perceive the world • Help them learn from mistakes, failures and success • Praise their efforts to learn • Positively correct undesirable behaviours • Be firm that they carry out their responsibilities

support of their complex and difficult role. Unless parents resolve their own emotional, social, intellectual, creative and sexual issues, they are unlikely to be able to effectively meet their responsibilities towards their children.

It is beyond the brief of this book to elaborate on parents' responsibilities towards children.* But what needs to be emphasised is that when parents find themselves frequently and intensely failing in their responsibilities, they must seek help, training and support.

❑ *Children's responsibilities towards parents*

The earlier children are made aware that they have responsibilities towards their parents the better. Some parents spoil children in the early years and suddenly expect them to be responsible in their adolescent years. Children need to be guided firmly and gently into seeing that their parents have rights and needs which must be respected and upheld. In their earlier years insisting on simple responsibilities – such as tidying away toys, washing and dressing themselves, appropriate table manners and making requests rather than commanding – goes a long way to preparing for greater responsibilities later on in life. It is crucial that parents do not allow children slide out of these responsibilities. The foundation of children's respect for others is the respect they show to their parents; this will also determine the respect they have for themselves.

Children's responsibilities towards parents	
• Respect their physical, emotional, sexual, social, creative and intellectual integrity • Love and respect them • Respond positively to reasonable requests • Listen to them	• Respect and take due care of family property and possessions • Address parents by preferred title • Be on time for meals • Communicate in respectful, direct and clear ways

* These issues are addressed in the author's books, *Self-Esteem: The Key to Your Child's Education* (Dublin: Gill & Macmillan, 1996) and *The Family: Love It and Leave It* (Dublin: Gill & Macmillan, 1996).

The more responsible children are in the home, the more responsible they are in schools and communities; the converse is also true. Parents have a major responsibility to ensure that their children take seriously their responsibilities towards them.

❑ *Children's responsibilities towards each other*

A relatively unchartered area is the effect of children's under-controlled or over-controlled behaviour on each other. The literature on bullying in schools has highlighted the devas-tating results on children who are victims of such behaviour. What has not been highlighted is the effects of the failure of children to stand up for each other's rights. The earlier that children in homes, schools and communities are educated in their responsibilities towards each other, the better chance there is of the development of mutual caring among children. Clearly, the nature and number of responsibilities increase as children get older.

Children's responsibilities towards each other	
• Respect each other's physical, emotional, sexual, social, cre-ative and intellectual integrity • Love and respect each other • Communicate in direct and clear ways • Break the silence on any physical, emotional or	sexual abuse of a peer to an adult who will listen and act • Respect and take care of each other's belongings • Address each other by first name • Listen to each other

❑ *Students' responsibilities towards teachers*

The actions of students play a significant part in determining whether or not the rights of teachers are met. Students need to be reminded frequently of their responsibilities towards teachers, which are part of the process that ensures teachers' rights and, indeed, their own rights are upheld. If a student disagrees with any of these responsibilities, then he needs to talk over his difficulties with parents and teachers. Most of all, he needs to know that any disrespect of the teacher or, indeed, of any other member of the school will not be tolerated.

Students' responsibilities towards teachers	
• Address them by their preferred title • Listen to them • Be on time for class • Walk into classroom in an orderly manner • Bring to school books and materials needed for class work • Respond positively to reasonable requests • Sit quietly during class • Attend to class activities	• Speak in turn in class • Complete reasonable homework assignments • Ask for help when work is difficult • Apologise when something unacceptable is said or done • Communicate distress directly and clearly to class teacher • Consult the committees that safeguard students' rights if distress goes unheeded

❏ *Teachers' responsibilities towards students*

The source of a good number of discipline problems is the attitudes and responses of teachers towards students. Teachers

Teachers' responsibilities towards students	
• Ensure that learning has only positive associations • Do not project own needs onto students • Treat a student's ill-disciplined conduct as saying something about that student, not about the teacher (see Chapters 4 and 14) • Make efforts to stay calm and relaxed at all times • Be fair, consistent and predictable in responses to all students • Place emphasis on effort rather than performance • Frequently praise academic and social efforts and affirm students	• Be positively firm in the face of difficult behaviour from students • Listen to all sides • Prepare lessons well • Be student-centred rather than programme-centred • Do not get trapped into conflict with a student presenting either under-controlled or over-controlled behaviours • Apologise for own ill-disciplined actions • Employ mistakes and failures as stepping-stones to further learning

have the responsibility to actively respect and respond to the rights of students in the same way as teachers want students to respect and respond to their rights. Practice of these responsibilities will certainly lead to a major decrease in discipline problems and will also act as a means of preventing the development of other problems. In exercising their responsibilities towards students, teachers need to recognise that the 'how' is more important than the 'what' of teaching.*

❑ *Teachers' responsibilities towards each other*

Whilst the number and variety of roles that a teacher is now expected to perform is one of the major sources of stress in teaching, a close runner-up is staff relationships. Cohesiveness, support, understanding, good morale, shared responsibility, openness and safety to be vulnerable are characteristics of a healthy staff. Regrettably, such a staff is more the exception than the rule. In many ways this is not surprising as staff development, staff morale and the rights and needs of teachers have not been regarded as central to the school system. By contrast, private industry is much more aware of the necessity of prioritising the needs of staff and is much more likely to recognise that a healthy staff is far more motivated, creative and productive.

In an unhealthy staff the members may experience distrust of each other, hostility, fear, lack of sensitivity, poor co-operation, criticism, cliques, poor leadership, and authoritarianism or passivity. If staff members do not support each other, particularly in terms of asserting and upholding their legitimate rights and needs, they can hardly reasonably expect other members of the school system to do so. Leaders play a vital role in establishing staff cooperation. However, teachers cannot afford to wait for others to take up the crusade for their rights. Each teacher is responsible for her own rights and must be determined to continually communicate them at the staff table to enable them to be acknowledged and acted upon.

---

* These issues are addressed in the author's book, *A Different Kind of Teacher* (Dublin: Gill & Macmillan, 1996).

It certainly makes a major difference when all teachers are willing to give their backing to the assertion of their rights. It is even more powerful when the school leaders lend their weight to the vindication of teachers' rights.

Teachers' responsibilities towards each other	
• Regularly affirm each other • Encourage each other's professional efforts • Request regular staff meetings • Listen to each other • Respect differences in opinion • Voice unmet needs • Cooperate with agreed school policies • Consistently and predictably apply school policies	• Admit when having difficulties with students or colleagues or school policies • Be supportive when a colleague is under pressure • Assist a colleague when help is genuinely needed • Positively confront unacceptable behaviours of colleagues • When grievances go unheeded, seek help outside the staff group

Affirmation is the genuine demonstration of regard for the unique person of another. It is the acknowledgment of the value of the presence of the other. It is the kind of caring and concern for another human being that you would rightly expect for yourself. Affirmation is an essential aspect of any human relationship, and its absence can leave teachers feeling invisible, unimportant and valueless.

Encouragement is the breath that gives life to the multiple tasks that teachers take on daily. Praise, appreciation and admiration of teachers' dedication need to be frequent responses for good staff morale to be engendered.

Regular staff meetings are an essential forum for teachers to voice their needs and grievances, but such voicing is only likely to occur in a safe emotional atmosphere which is characterised by listening, acceptance of differences, kindness towards vulnerability, support, understanding and a willingness to help. It is crucial that staff meetings are structured and meaningful. Agendas that are not imposed but instead spring from the needs of staff are much more likely to lead to lively and productive meetings. Rescheduling of partially resolved or unresolved issues is necessary until a resolution is found.

Active listening to the other's joys, wishes, requests, worries and vulnerability is one of the most powerful means of showing respect to a colleague. It does not mean having to agree with what the other person is saying but it does mean respecting her enough to want to know about her unique experiences and what, if any, help or support is needed.

Differences in opinion are the creative life-blood of a staff; conformity leads only to apathy and stagnation. Differences do not mean opposition but rather present options for a staff group to consider. A possible compromise is to test a particular option for a period of time, whilst not losing sight of other presented possibilities.

Cooperation among teachers on agreed school policies is necessary if teachers are to present a united front to students, parents and management with regard to the importance of their rights and the necessity of upholding them.

Consistency and predictability have long been recognised as the hallmarks of effective discipline systems. When there is inconsistency within and between teachers and unpredictability in the application of school policies, students do not know where the boundaries lie and will continue to push until they find them. In such an inconsistent and unpredictable school system, what will prevail is either unbridled licence for students to do as they will or a chaotic regime that swings from sternness to 'anything goes'; everybody loses out, most of all teachers.

When any teacher is experiencing difficulties, be they personal, interpersonal or professional, it is incumbent on colleagues to be concerned. One teacher's difficulties can send a ripple or indeed a big wave across the calm sea of an effectively functioning school. Students who are distressed by a particular teacher's disrespectful, authoritarian or cynical approach may carry their unresolved feelings of rage and anger not only into another teacher's class, but also into the schoolyard, community and home. The ethos of the school can also suffer, particularly when the 'reputation' of such teachers spreads throughout the community. There are always deep psychological and social reasons why certain teachers operate in this way, but ignoring the behaviour does nothing to help either the teachers or the students who suffer at their hands or the parents who have to cope with students who learn to hate school.

The ideal situation is where the teacher herself admits to her difficulties and seeks the help and support she needs. When this does not occur, perhaps because of fear of judgment, it falls to colleagues, management and parents to confront the unacceptable behaviour. Confrontation is an act of caring and as such needs to demonstrate understanding, compassion and a willingness to provide help and support. It must also show firmness that other people in the school system will not be put at risk because of the vulnerability of the teacher. If caring confrontation goes unheeded, then help from outside the school system is required. The bottom line must be that no stone will remain unturned until the situation is resolved.

❑ *Teachers' responsibilities towards principals*

The responsibilities teachers have towards each other also apply in their relationship with their principal. Teachers have the following additional responsibilities towards principals:

- Respond to the legitimate rights and needs of principals
- Recognise and respect the roles of principals
- Communicate directly and clearly any dissatisfaction with leadership
- Attend and contribute to staff meetings
- When unheeded, go beyond principal for whatever help is required

Passivity is an all too frequent characteristic of relationships between staff members and principals, resulting in serious discipline issues being left unspoken and unheeded. It is essential that a climate of safety be created so that teachers and principals can voice to each other their concerns, resentments and needs.

It may seem strange to say that a teacher has the responsibility to go over a principal's head when the need arises. However, principals are largely the architects of school morale and effectiveness, and, as much for their own sakes as that of the other members of the system, poor leadership cannot go unconfronted.

❑ *Principals' responsibilities towards teachers*

Ineffective leadership is a much quoted cause of stress in teaching. Leadership requires a set of skills that are additional to teaching skills. There are some school principals who are dominant, rigid and do not listen to the rights and needs of their staff and others who hide away in the office for fear of confrontation or conflict. There are still others who can be threatening and manipulative. All of these managers need

Principals' responsibilities towards teachers	
• Regularly meet each member of staff	• Be open to feedback on style of leadership
• Recognise, appreciate and encourage their contributions	• If required, seek further training in management
• Listen to their needs	• Delegate responsibilities fairly
• Confront those who are not meeting their responsibilities	• Hold regular staff meetings
• Be open to differences of opinion	• Organise meaningful agendas for staff meetings
• Be approachable and available	• Consult on school policies
• Be supportive	• Develop, through consultation with teachers, students and parents, a school mission statement and operational and discipline policies
• When deemed fair, provide help and back-up when requested	
• Be direct and clear on expectations of them	• Confront parents of children who are not showing responsible behaviour
• Foster group decision-making	• When needed, seek help

help to move away from these ineffective leadership approaches towards a more transformational type of leadership. If a school principal is not ready to take on such a responsibility, then it becomes a matter of urgency that the staff demand more effective leadership; and if this is not forthcoming, they must then seek help outside the school system. Structures need to be created for such a process, as much for the teachers and students as for the principal involved. An educational system that allows and colludes with poor leadership is neglectful of all members of the system.

Some of the responsibilities of school principals towards teachers are similar to those involved in teacher–teacher relationships. Those that are specific to the role of manager include being available, approachable, confrontative, supportive and helpful. There are many principals who balk at confronting a teacher who is not fulfilling her responsibilities. They may be fearful of conflict or of upsetting the teacher, but when they let a staff member slide out of responsibility, they fail themselves, the teacher who is not coping, the other teachers and the students. Equally, everybody in the system is failed when a principal does not seek help and support from parents of children who are not adapting to the school system and who, through their undisciplined behaviours, are causing undue stress to teachers and other students.

Fair delegation of responsibilities is the mark of a good leader. However, there are some principals who, due to their own fears of failure and criticism, feel they have to do everything themselves. Staff members will not feel affirmed and their efforts will not be recognised by this kind of manager. There are others who are too quick to pass the buck of responsibility to avoid being held accountable for any difficulties that may arise. The effective manager is in touch with the skills and motivational levels of the different teachers and will delegate by matching the responsibility to the particular attributes of individual teachers. Such a manager keeps a keen eye on workloads to ensure no teacher is either overburdened or underutilised.

A good principal recognises the necessity of consultation and group decision-making. Where there are large staff groups, subgroups may need to be formed to ensure that the voice of each teacher is heard. Managers need to keep a watchful eye on teachers who are not coping and be ready to offer help and support in a discreet way. It is vital not to judge the teacher's actions but to approach the situation with understanding, concern and compassion. This approach is much more likely to bear the fruit of personal and professional development on the part of the teacher who is stressed.

Social systems are far more efficient and effective when there is a clear mission statement and clear operational and discipline policies. Regular review of these is wise, as the culture of the school, like the wider society, is in a continual state of flux. However, changes can be better accommodated when a system has the stability of clear expectations and accountability.

If parents are not meeting their responsibilities either towards their children or towards teachers, it is essential that the school principal and board of management confront them. Lack of confrontation by principals means that the rights of both students and teachers continue to be jeopardised. Parents need to know very definitely that the management of the school will not tolerate any infringement of the rights of teachers by students.

School principals have the task of ensuring that the rights of all involved in the school system are upheld. This involves a very difficult balancing act and accordingly school principals can experience serious stress levels. Some principals are now seeking support from colleagues but stronger demands on school inspectors and government are needed also. This is not to say that principals should not look to themselves to resolve stressful situations; but having done this and having corrected failures in leadership, they must seek help outside themselves in the resolution of remaining problems. This is an act of strength; those who do not admit to weaknesses in themselves or in their school system block healthy development.

❏ *Teachers' responsibilities towards parents*

Education must be seen as a shared responsibility between teachers and parents. Indeed it is time that teachers reduced the level of responsibility they take for students and insisted on parents taking their fair share.

Teachers' responsibilities towards parents	
• Accept their role in their children's education • Listen to their concerns • Contact them when their children persistently show either under-controlled or over-controlled behaviours • Give them professional advice on their children's education	• Be supportive of those who are experiencing major difficulties with their children • Communicate in respectful, clear and direct ways • Acquaint them with teachers' own rights and limitations • Set up formal and informal means of contact

Parents can feel threatened when requested to come to the school because of a child's ill-disciplined behaviour. Parents can also be nervous when they themselves want to approach a teacher or principal with concerns about their child's academic progress or with complaints from their child about aggressive or passive behaviours on the part of a teacher. It is necessary for teachers to be sensitive to the vulnerabilities of parents and to create an atmosphere of safety when parents come to meet them.

❏ *Parents' responsibilities towards teachers*

Parents must make it easy for teachers to approach them about their children's educational progress and any discipline problems that may arise. Parents need to see teachers as being valuing and caring of their children and as requiring their help to help with children's learning within the school. Through regular meetings, a joint approach can be developed. Where there are two parents or guardians, it is important that not just one (usually the mother) but both of them attend these meetings. It is important that parents and teachers set up, in a caring way, a fair system of responsibility for the child and that agreed ways of relating to the child and demands for responsible behaviour are followed through predictably and consistently in the home and in the classroom. When a child needs to go to some outside agency (for example, clinical psychologist, educational psychologist, family therapist, social worker, counsellor), this must be done in a strictly confidential manner.

Parents' responsibilities towards teachers	
• Share responsibility for the education and behavioural management of children • Attend parent–teacher meetings • Respond positively to requests for help from teachers • When children are encountering difficulties in school, listen to all sides	• Cooperate with teachers in the development of responsible behaviour on the part of children within the school • When requested, seek the help of helping agencies outside the school

There are some parents who believe their children can do no wrong and others (less so now) who believe teachers are always right. Both assumptions are misguided and it is wise that parents learn to listen to all sides.

CHAPTER 7

Empowerment of Children, Parents and Teachers

❏ *What empowerment means*
  - A strong sense of self
  - Social and emotional competence
  - Knowledge and training in your area of responsibility
    - ➭ **Teachers**
    - ➭ **Parents**
    - ➭ **Children**
  - Assertiveness
  - Openness to questioning and being questioned
  - A celebration of differences
  - Autonomy

❏ *What empowerment means*

It has been seen that over-controlled behaviour is as much a contributor to discipline problems as is under-controlled behaviour. Adults and children who are, for example, passive, overpleasing, timid or fearful lack the personal power to take control of aspects of their own lives and to confront violations of their rights; they require empowerment. Empowerment is also necessary for the perpetrators of under-controlled behaviour, as they lack self-control and respect for others and they strongly attempt to control others.

An essential aspect of any discipline system is to create a culture wherein victims and perpetrators of ill-disciplined behaviours are empowered both personally and interpersonally. Personal empowerment is developed through a recognition of your own uniqueness and vast intellectual potential and through the acquisition of knowledge and skills. Interpersonal empowerment is the ability to hold onto one's own respect for self and ways of being in this world in the face of pressure to conform to the ways of others. People who are empowered do not tolerate violations of their own or others' rights. However, their vindication of rights is done in a way that does not threaten the rights of the perpetrators.

Up to recent times, empowerment of individuals had not been a marked characteristic of discipline in our social and religious systems. Typically, the Christian and other churches enforced discipline through domination and fear, and certainly did not give people a sense of their goodness, value, worth and capability. In homes and schools, parents and teachers also ruled largely by fear and control: children were to be seen and not heard. The adults in these social systems had considerable power, but it was a power that came not from a sense of respect for themselves or others, but from a position of authority. You dare not contradict the head of the family! Teachers and clergy belonged to the educated class and were put on pedestals and no parent or child would question their authority.

Fortunately, teachers and clergy have fallen from their pedestals, but many of them are struggling with the empowered position that parents and children are developing. The fact that many are not coping with being critically examined and questioned indicates that the power they exercised to date was pseudo, as a person with real power is not threatened by difference or questioning. Likewise, parents, particularly those who were authoritarian and rigid in approach, are having difficulties in dealing with their now more empowered children.

Respect for self and others is a key aspect of both personal and interpersonal empowerment and is central to the discipline philosophy outlined already in this book. Other aspects of empowerment are:

- A strong sense of self
- Social and emotional competence
- Knowledge and training in your area of responsibility
- Assertiveness
- Openness to questioning and being questioned
- A celebration of differences
- Autonomy

■ A strong sense of self

A strong sense of self is the cornerstone of effective discipline. When teachers, parents or children have a strong feeling about their own goodness, uniqueness, capability and worth and they carry this sense of self into their relationships with self and others, they are automatically self-disciplined, fair and firm in asserting their own needs and expectations of others and they will not tolerate any disrespect. The contrary is also true: when teachers, parents or children have poor self-esteem, they carry that poor sense of self into everything they do and are easily threatened by failure, criticism and undisciplined behaviours. To protect themselves from further hurt they will often resort to aggression or passivity. Such responses do nothing to resolve the difficult behaviours and their continuance is more likely.

As an adult your sense of self is grounded in your own relationship with yourself. In the case of children the sense of self is determined by how parents, teachers and other significant adults relate to them. When that relating is generally warm, affirming, unconditional, accepting, nurturing, valuing, respectful, supportive, challenging, humorous, encouraging and firm, children will emerge with a secure sense of self. However, if the relationship for the most part is characterised by irritability, dismissiveness, conditionality, harshness, aggression, passivity, criticism, ridicule, scoldings, hurtful labelling and comparisons with others, then children will develop an image of self that mirrors all these hurtful messages. Children have to depend on adults to provide the fertile soil for the growth of a positive sense of self. But adults cannot afford to wait around for others to be accepting of them, and must take on this responsibility for themselves.

The relationship with self is the most unconsidered of all relationships, even though its nature determines how you are in relationships with others. As an adult you need to become your own best parent and to daily interact with self in a way a loving parent would with children. This is an issue that none of us can afford to ignore. The responsibility for the loving care of yourself sits squarely on your own shoulders, and

must be taken on by you so that you do not burden others –
adults or children – with the responsibility for your welfare.
The responsibility we have to respect one another does not
contradict this necessity to own your own responsibility to
care for yourself. When others are not responsive to your
legitimate needs, you have no right to force them to uphold
your rights, but you do have a responsibility to continue to
look for means to safeguard them.

■ Social and emotional competence

Children develop emotional and social competence from their
experience of how adults relate to them. Parents and teachers
are the primary models of such competence and their level of
ability will in turn largely determine children's ability in this
vital area of human functioning. Regrettably, men still tend to
be uncomfortable with emotional expression and it is important
that this unhealthy legacy does not continue to be passed on
to children.

Parents and teachers must teach children to identify, understand and express their feelings in respectful ways. Many
children bottle up their feelings or express them aggressively.
Either form of expression will leave children with blocked
needs. Feelings arise to alert us to the presence of needs: needs
for love, comfort, nurturance, understanding, encouragement,
choice and affirmation. When we are out of touch with our
feelings, we carry a host of unmet needs inside ourselves.

Modelling the expression of both welfare and emergency
feelings by parents and teachers is the most effective way of
developing children's emotional literacy. Welfare feelings
indicate that our important needs are being met and include
feelings of security, warmth, love, compassion, joy and enthu-
siasm. Emergency feelings are those which alert us to unmet
needs and include fear, anger, sadness, loneliness, depression,
hurt, anxiety and insecurity. For example, if a child comes
home from school quiet and non-communicative, it is wise for
parents to explore in a non-invasive way what may be troubling
him. It is important for the parents not to ask a closed question:
'what is wrong with you?'; instead ask an open question or

make an open statement such as 'I feel there might be some-thing troubling you and I want you to know I'm here to listen and to help'. The tone of voice and facial expression that accompany the verbal message determine whether the child will feel safe enough to respond to the invitation to talk.

Adults also need to model for children how to respond positively to the expressed feelings of others. There are adults who show distinct discomfort in response to the expression of love, warmth, affirmation or joy and react strongly to expres-sions of anger, sadness, upset or anxiety. When children witness such reactions they learn to inhibit their feelings. Parents and teachers need to demonstrate genuine and active listening to expressed feelings and positive firmness to any aggressive or manipulative means of dealing with feelings.

▪ Knowledge and training in your area of responsibility

↬ Teachers

When any profession is involved in the caring, teaching or holistic development of children, adolescents or adults, it is expedient that an integral part of their training involves devel-oping the capacity to understand fully their charges. In the case of teachers, their training provides a knowledge base and consequent power base, but if teachers are to maintain a professional power base, the limitations of their initiation into teaching need to be recognised. Much of previous teacher training focused too heavily on 'what to teach' but not enough on 'how to teach'. The 'how' is a much more difficult process and requires not only knowledge of effective teaching methods but also a good working understanding of human behaviour. The areas of knowledge that teachers need to understand if they are to survive and adapt to a rapidly changing wider culture and develop effective discipline systems are:

- Child, adolescent and adult development
- Development of self-esteem of children and adults
- Motivation
- Holistic approaches to learning difficulties
- Human sexuality

- Interpersonal dynamics
- Emotional, social, intellectual, creative and behavioural problems of children and adults
- Communication
- Group dynamics
- Problem-solving
- Stress management
- Management
- Leadership

An even more pressing requirement for professionals is the healing of their own vulnerability, or at least an understanding of and an attempt at resolving hurts of the past. Too many adults bring the baggage of their past emotional wounds and present insecurities into their roles and load children with their vulnerabilities. The cycle of neglect is thereby perpetuated. The need for broader and longer initial training and for ongoing training of teachers must be taken on board by colleges of education and by government. School principals may complain that there is no time in the school calendar for staff development. But it is a failure of leadership not to recognise that the teacher who has a strong feeling of both personal and professional power is far more effective in the classroom.

↪ Parents

If teachers have fared poorly in the knowledge stakes, parents have been even more neglected. Parenting is the most difficult profession of all. It demands round-the-clock responsibility for the emotional, social, sexual, physical, educational, career, recreational, spiritual and sensual development of children. All of this without any formal training! Even though the state pays considerable lip service to the sanctity and importance of the family in society, it has given neither the money nor the necessary training for parents that would reflect this value.

There are some parents who, through reading, mature reflection on their own life experience and attendance at privately run parenting courses, have developed some knowledge of effective parenting skills. However, these tend to be in the minority. Also in the minority are those parents who have healed the wounds of their own childhoods and come to a more compassionate and loving place of self-development and understanding of others. It is well known among teachers that the students who are persistently difficult inevitably come from insecure and troubled homes. If it is to be successful, any intervention has to involve the parents of these students.

If parents are to become more empowered, they need formal training in such areas as:

- Parenting
- Child development
- Personal development
- Sexual development
- Self-esteem
- Emotional, behavioural and social problems of children
- Basic teaching skills
- Communication
- Problem-solving

⇨ Children

Like teachers and parents, children too must have opportunities to develop the knowledge necessary to cope with their particular responsibilities. Adults may unwisely assume that children will develop such areas of knowledge naturally. Children need to be given knowledge in areas such as:

- How to concentrate
- How to study
- How to learn from mistakes
- How to ask for help
- How to use their bodies intelligently (in sports, mechanical skills, woodwork)
- How to use public services (transport, telephone)
- How to use and express their feelings
- How to communicate
- How to solve problems

- Hygiene
- How to cook, clean, tidy
- How to look after their clothes

Children who are well versed in their areas of responsibility adapt to and cope more effectively with the school environment than those not given such competence.

■ Assertiveness

The engine of empowerment is the ability to assert your rights, needs, misgivings, opinions and grievances. People who are assertive have a presence that is tangible but not threatening. They express themselves clearly and strongly but in a way that listens to and respects the other person's point of view. Assertiveness stems from an acceptance of self and others and a respect for the equal right of each person to be different in their needs and opinions. Assertiveness is very different from aggression, which reflects the belief that might is right and one person has the right to control and dominate another. Assertiveness is also different from passivity which arises from the belief that 'I don't count, but everybody else does'. Assertiveness is based on the fundamental human principle that each person counts.

People who are assertive take responsibility for their own issues and do not attempt to load them onto others. Assertiveness means communicating directly and clearly on matters that affect your life and, sometimes, the lives of others. As regards the latter, it is sad when adults 'turn a blind eye' to the abuse of children or of other adults. Alongside aggression and violence, passivity is the greatest disease in any social system. Passivity is as neglectful of people's physical, emotional and social welfare as is aggression. Passivity can operate at a personal level whereby you protectively choose to ignore, bury or dilute your own rights and needs or to accept neglect or abuse from others of these same rights and needs. It can also function at an interpersonal level when you do nothing about the neglect and abuse of others.

Teachers have been slow to request management or colleagues to respect and uphold their rights in the face of disruptive behaviours on the part of a child or class. These teachers will say they feel it is an act of weakness to admit to being unable to control a child or a class, but the hidden issue is that they are fearful of ridicule should they ask for help. This dependence cripples their assertiveness. Nowadays children are considerably more empowered and teachers need all the help they can get to uphold their rights. The ability to assert their rights as carers is vital to their survival and their enjoyment of their demanding profession.

Parents too have been slow to assert their rights and the rights of their children in the face of unacceptable behaviour on the part of teachers. Parents will say that they worry that confrontation might result in their child being more victimised by the targeted teacher, but the real issue is that they are fearful for themselves. They fear not being able to hold their own with the teacher and ending up feeling humiliated and embarrassed. Children also can be afraid to assert their rights or can attempt to block parents championing their rights as they too can fear retaliation from teachers or peers. Children and parents need support to understand that the non-assertion of their rights, because of fear of aggravating the abuse situation, will only lead to a worsening of the situation. Non-assertiveness is tantamount to giving control of yourself over to another.

Modelling of assertiveness is a key responsibility for teachers and parents, not only for their own empowerment but even more so for that of children. Children who are assertive have a good sense of self, are clear on their rights and needs, and will not accept abuse from teachers, parents and peers.

Rigidity can be a major challenge to the development of effective discipline systems. People who are rigid tend to be pushy and dominant and to blame others for their unmet rights and needs. Moreover, there are children who are victims of inflexible parenting and teaching, and teachers who are at the mercy of rigid colleagues or principals. Unless these personal barriers are removed, progress on discipline procedures is unlikely.

- Openness to questioning and being questioned

A strong index of maturity and personal empowerment is openness to change; it involves regular questioning of your own views on all aspects of life and also valuing others' challenge to your beliefs. Rigidity, fundamentalism, dismissal of others' opinions and labelling of others are strong indications of deep emotional insecurity and dependence on others. The need to be always right is a cry for acceptance and a fear of being wrong. Until people learn to accept themselves and embrace failure as a wonderful means to further learning, they will continue to rely on rigidity as their protection against rejection.

Openness does not mean being like the chameleon that changes its colour to blend with its environment. Openness means giving considered attention to the contrary opinions of others and a willingness to change yours when there are sound reasons for doing so.

- A celebration of differences

Western culture is emerging from a past that reinforced sameness and punished difference. Churches, schools and homes rewarded conformity to their mores and were greatly threatened by any opposing ideas. Once differences do not threaten basic human rights, then they are best seen as means of challenging or widening perspectives on all aspects of life. In homes and schools where differences are celebrated, all members of these systems will have a high level of self-esteem and will feel freed to explore what is best for them as individuals in all areas of living. Individuality and respect for others mark the people who live in social systems where differences are cherished.

For adults who are emotionally insecure, difference is viewed as opposition and rejection, and may be greeted with harsh treatment or withdrawal. These adults will not be able to accept differences until they have first resolved their own personal insecurities.

- Autonomy

Freedom to be self, to live life in ways unique to self, to be non-conformist and to resist the imposition by others of artificial values and goals is the apex of empowerment. Such autonomy is possible only when the other aspects of empowerment are firmly in place. It is a goal to which all adults can aspire and one which needs to be fostered in children. The achievement of autonomy is the fountain of infinite productivity, creativity, self-fulfilment and fruitful relationships with others. It is regrettable that many social systems are threatened by autonomous individuals. Ironically, the greatest threat to the welfare of any social system is conformity.

CHAPTER 8

Safeguarding Children's Rights

❑ *Creating structures that safeguard rights*
❑ *Safeguarding the rights of children*
❑ *Safeguarding children's rights in the home*
  ▪ Permission to voice violations
  ▪ Regular family meetings
  ▪ Family handbook
  ▪ Sanctions to safeguard children's rights
  ▪ 'Safe room' for children
  ▪ Back-up support systems outside the home
  ▪ Choosing effective childminders
❑ *Safeguarding students' rights in the school*
  ▪ Student committee
  ▪ Student handbook
  ▪ Start-of-year meeting of student committee
  ▪ Regular meetings of student committee
  ▪ Sanctions to safeguard students' rights
  ▪ Back-up support systems inside and outside of school
  ▪ Structures common to both students and teachers
    ➪ **Morning assembly**
    ➪ **School handbook and classroom notice-boards**
    ➪ **Discipline committee**
    ➪ **Sanction room**

❑ *Creating structures that safeguard rights*

The declaration of rights and the statement of responsibilities in themselves are not sufficient to guarantee that the rights of children, parents and teachers are vindicated. Certainly the empowerment of individuals makes it more likely that their rights will be respected and acted upon, but empowerment itself does not necessarily lead to social structures that endorse and support the rights of people. For example, a married woman who has developed a good sense of herself and who is strongly in touch with her rights to safety, love and respect may have her rights violated by her spouse. This could happen because women do not often have a safe haven to go to when their rights are neglected. What is needed then are structures within homes, schools and communities which ensure that the rights of all who live in these social systems are valued, respected and safeguarded. Definite structures not only enshrine the declaration of rights and their accompanying responsibilities but ensure strong and clear actions that endorse and maintain rights when these are under threat.

Sanctions are frequently implemented when rights are threatened. It is essential to see that sanctions are not invented to punish individuals who transgress the rights of others, but are employed entirely to safeguard rights. For example, the heavy fines imposed for dangerous driving are designed to get the driver to slow down so that the right of the rest of us to feel safe driving on the roads is safeguarded. If the driver sees it as a punishment, he is more likely to feel resentful and less likely to slow down. Making sure all concerned understand the safeguarding purpose of sanctions is vital to effective discipline systems.

The creation of structures that safeguard rights is not a simple process: it demands time, commitment, creativity and resources. To date, homes and schools have not placed enough emphasis on nor given sufficient time to the creation of safety for their members. Discipline is a philosophy that needs to permeate all interactions, and as such demands equal place with the parenting and educating of children. Curriculum requirements all too often cripple the attempts of teachers to create an effective discipline system. It is necessary that adequate time be allocated during the school day to the creation and maintenance of safety for everybody.

❑ *Safeguarding the rights of children*

No discipline system can survive double standards: people in authority must accept that children have similar rights to themselves and must acknowledge that they can and do violate these rights. Measures to safeguard children's rights are needed in the school and home, and these safeguarding structures need to be both visible and powerful. Furthermore, when the rights of children are not upheld by either teachers or parents, sanctions need to be available to children to reinstate the violated rights and safeguard against further neglect. The availability of sanctions to children is the sanctuary that maintains their well-being. It is astounding how adults can be quick to respond with a sanction when a child displays under-controlled behaviour – 'he should be grounded' or 'he deserves a telling off' or 'I know what he needs' – but when it comes to their own loss of control, adults can be slow to accept the imposition of sanctions. Of course, teachers and parents need to recognise that sanctions are not designed to get at them, but have the express purpose of upholding the rights of children.

When children witness teachers accepting sanctions as just responses to behaviours that threaten the emotional, physical, intellectual or social safety of their students, they are more likely to accept the necessity also of sanctions to safeguard the rights of teachers. After all, children learn most of the ways they behave from observation of adults, particularly parents and teachers.

❑ Safeguarding children's rights in the home

It is a sad fact that most violations of the rights of children occur within the home. Children who persistently create problems within schools and communities inevitably come from troubled homes. While recognising that neglect is never deliberately perpetrated by parents, nevertheless its continuance cannot be tolerated. Compared with the not too distant past, there are now many sources of help available to parents who are not parenting effectively. Also, the partnership between schools and homes which is now developing offers greater possibilities, not only for addressing the neglect of children's rights in the home but also for healing hurts experienced. There is an African saying, 'it takes a village to raise a child'. It can no longer be acceptable that people ignore known neglect of children. Children need as many sentinels as possible to watch over their rights. The more children live in a safe world where their physical, emotional, social, intellectual, sexual and spiritual rights are treasured and safeguarded, the more they thrive in all aspects of living and develop into mature, self-motivated and self-reliant individuals.

There are many expressions of violation of children's rights but the most important medium of neglect is the relationship that exists between parents and children. An unchartered area is the effects of childminders on children. The relationship between child and child within the home can also lead to violation of rights, but it is a failure of parenting that allows such relating to persist.

The most common type of relating between parents and children is the dominating and controlling one, where children are loved only when they conform to the demands of parents. Whether the demands are reasonable or unreasonable, love must not be a weapon used by parents to uphold their rights. Certainly, parents, like teachers and students, need to find ways of vindicating their rights, but violating the right of children to be loved is neither desirable nor effective. This is an issue that parents cannot afford to ignore; to do so means dooming children to lives of insecurity, fear and dependence.

The second most common type of relating between parents and children is one where the children are overprotected and deprived of the necessary opportunities to become independent and self-reliant. These parents rarely send messages of belief and trust in their children because too many things are done for them. They rob children of confidence and competence. These children learn that it is safer to stay helpless, because to assert their rights to be themselves, to be different, to exercise choice and to be independent would mean risking the most threatening experience of all – the withdrawal of love. In this situation, love once again is the means employed to gain control over children. These parents are so dependent on being needed as a way of gaining love and recognition that they infect their children with their own vulnerability.

Unfortunately, some children come from families where, no matter what they do, they cannot gain love. In such families there is either gross lack of love and nurturing or gross physical, emotional, social or sexual abuse. The rights of children are neither heard nor seen in these homes, and are horribly violated. The parents in such families are in dire need of help to redeem their lost selves but the question must be asked: who now takes care of the children? Ways must be found to save the children from the bottomless pit of having no sense of being loved and wanted. If solutions are not found, the consequences are delinquency, drug addiction, alcoholism, violence, depression, troubled marriages and families, and utter dependence on social systems.

The prime right of children (indeed of all humans) is love: love is a sacred right which nothing must threaten. Naturally, most parents are concerned to foster responsible behaviours in their children but they will be more effective in achieving this if they:

- Create an unconditional, loving relationship with their children
- Request rather than order children to do things
- Believe in and trust children to learn to do for themselves
- Set realistic physical, emotional, social and educational challenges
- Model the behaviours they wish their children to adopt
- Impose sanctions in a loving and firm way when legitimate rights and needs are not being respected
- Apologise when they lose control with their children's behaviour
- Are supportive and encouraging when children take on challenges

There are no parents who do not lose control with children now and again, but once they apologise and heal the rift in the relationship, such lapses do not have any lasting effect on children's welfare. It is the persistent neglect of their rights that poses serious blocks to children's development.

The rights of children that are most likely to be neglected within homes are:

- The right to unconditional love
- The right to feel wanted
- The right to positive experiences

- The right to be communicated with in direct and clear ways
- The right to be listened to
- The right to fairness
- The right to be different
- The right to be challenged
- The right to choice
- The right to independence
- The right to fail and make mistakes

There are few structures within homes to enable children safeguard their rights. In our culture children have not been empowered to stand up for their rights. Consequently, children use much of their energy, intelligence and creativity in attempts to countercontrol their parents and thereby do not achieve self-control. Neither has our culture created structures outside the home that could save children from the neglect they experience in the home. When parents are not able to parent effectively, others have to take on the responsibility for the children's overall welfare. Some progress in this regard has been made in the areas of physical and sexual abuse. However, the most enduring abuses are emotional and intellectual, and structures and systems to redeem children from these drowning pools have not yet been developed. Children themselves must not stand idly by when their rights are violated.

Structures to safeguard children's rights in the home	
• Listing of clearly defined rights of children (see Chapter 5) on prominent display	• Family handbook
	• Listing of clearly defined sanctions to safeguard children's rights
• Listing of clearly defined responsibilities of parents (see Chapter 6) on prominent display	• Creation of a 'safe room' for children
• Permission to voice violations	• Back-up support systems outside the home
• Regular family meetings	• Choosing effective childminders

Certainly, the American situation where children divorce their parents is the equivalent of using a sledge hammer to swat a fly. More appropriate means must be made available for children to safeguard their rights in less extreme cases of neglect. The higher the level of support they receive from adults to exercise those powers the better.

■ **Permission to voice violations**

The most potent structure for children to safeguard their rights is the permission to voice violations. This permission must be frequently on the lips of parents and other significant adults in children's lives. Children need to be told who they can approach when they are troubled. A parent needs to let a child know that, though he may be cross and insensitive at times, he loves her, and that he needs her to let him know when she is distressed by his behaviour. The parent can also give the child permission to talk to another adult – other parent, grandparent, uncle, aunt, teacher, family doctor, priest or neighbour.

■ **Regular family meetings**

Even before a child reaches the stage of verbal reasoning, a meeting between parents on how they are coping with meeting their child's rights is essential. Pre-school children so much depend on parents and others to be there for them and they are particularly vulnerable when their needs are not heeded. Clearly, levels of neglect vary and no parent can meet all the demands of children all of the time. In any case, children understand this falling short, once parents do it in ways that are loving and caring. Also parents must be caring of themselves and their rights and needs, and they must get support in the difficult task of parenting. It is important that from an early age children see that parents are separate from them, have their own identity and need their own time and space. It is very confusing for children when the boundaries between them and parents are blurred. Parents must aim to strike a balance between being respectful of their children's and their own rights. When parents lose control with their children, certainly the rights of the children must somehow be reinstated, but what the parents need most of all is understanding, support and tangible help – not judgment.

When there are two parents, the family meeting can serve the purpose of reviewing how the couple are with each other, how each partner is within themselves and how each is with the children. A review of the rights of children and the ensuing responsibilities of parents provides a good basis for discussion on how well the children's rights are being served. The meeting offers the opportunity for each parent to listen to and be supportive of the other. It is vital that an atmosphere of gentleness, caring and support is created. If that is not possible, then there are other serious issues that need to be examined: the relationship between the partners, the level of self-esteem of each one and the emotional baggage they may be carrying from their own families of origin.

Where there is a lone parent with pre-school children, that parent would be advised to find a good friend who can be his sounding board in terms of how he is coping with the children. Permission to be honest and open needs to be given to the friend; otherwise disclosure may be too threatening.

As soon as children develop competency in language they can become a party to the family meeting. Slowly but surely, using their current level of understanding and use of language, they can be informed of their rights, their parents' responsibilities and ways that they can safeguard their precious rights. They need to be frequently reminded that such caring works both ways.

Family meetings need to occur at least once weekly. Parents, like teachers, need to take the issue of discipline seriously and be willing to commit time, resources and creativity to its development in the home. Part of that commitment could be the writing of the family handbook.

■ Family handbook

The family handbook should be focused chiefly on the rights, responsibilities and safeguarding structures for each member of the family. Children can be encouraged to read these frequently (or have them read to them). Other matters that could be included are birthdays, special occasions, future plans, role and task allocations, and work and school responsibilities.

■ Sanctions to safeguard children's rights

Sanctions must be available to children just as they are to parents and teachers, and it is the responsibility of parents to acquaint children with the safeguarding sanctions they can employ in the home.

Sanctions to safeguard children's rights in the home	
• Make a positive and firm request of the parent to respect the violated right	(d) neighbour, (e) teacher, (f) family doctor or (g) member of clergy
• Make a request for an apology	• Report breach to designated person
• Leave unhappy situation and go to 'safe room'	• Leave the house and go to a named safe haven
• Request to talk to parent when parent has calmed down	• Refuse to return home until all threats have been removed
• Inform parent that the breach of right will be reported to one of the following: (a) other parent or guardian, (b) grandparent, (c) aunt or uncle,	• Contact 'Childline', the Irish Society for the Prevention of Cruelty to Children's telephone helpline
	• Go to local police station

This is not an exhaustive list of possible sanctions, but the principle involved is clear: children deserve to have recourse to actions that bring about an environment of safety when their security has been breached.

■ 'Safe room' for children

It is desirable that a particular room in the house be given the status of a 'safe room' where children can go when their rights are under attack. The parent who has violated the child's right must neither verbally nor physically pass the threshold of that room; otherwise it ceases to be what it is designed to be – safe.

- Back-up support systems outside the home

When children feel greatly threatened they may need to resort to a haven outside the home. Again this sanctuary needs to have been previously decided upon by the family so that when an undisciplined parent recovers his composure, he will know where his child has gone. Examples of agreed safe places are a neighbour's or relative's or priest's house or police station. The parent must respect that place and only enter it with the permission of the child. Once there, he must uphold the rights of his child.

When the level of threat to their security is very great, some children may refuse to return home. Parents must not fall into the trap of forcing the child home as this confirms the child's worst fears. In respecting and understanding the child's reluctance to return home the parent is clearly beginning to re-create that which has been lost – safety. Once the parent continues to pursue that goal the child will eventually return home.

As an aid to children's safety, the Childline telephone number could be included in the family handbook and visually displayed in the kitchen or a Childline card could be given to the children to have in their bedroom.

When there is physical violence, sexual abuse or, indeed, gross emotional abuse (shouting, hostile silences that can go on for days on end), children can seek the sanctuary of the local police station. Parents need to see that this action on the part of the child is not designed to embarrass them but is a loud cry from the heart of the child to be safe in the family.

- Choosing effective childminders

Nowadays children can spend more time with childminders than with parents, especially in the crucial formative stage from infancy to five years. Considerable thought needs to go into the selection of a childminder; unfortunately, too often convenience for the working parents is the criterion that determines choice. The well-being of the child is the central issue, and the parenting qualities of childminders should be decisive in choosing a minder.

Certainly, a recognised training in childminding would be a reassuring asset for a candidate to possess, but bear in mind that education does not automatically ensure maturity and the ability to care. Equally, do not assume that the most suitable person is a woman who has reared her own family. You would need a looking glass into the past to see how effective her parenting was. So a wise course of action is to work side by side with a childminder for a period of, say, a week and to observe her interaction with your children before you make a decision about employing the person.

Observation is far more reliable than interviews, diplomas, references, hearsay and curriculum vitae. Look for the qualities that will ensure children feel safe, loved, challenged, encouraged and positively corrected when they transgress boundaries. Patience, kindness, humour, flexibility, order and calmness are characteristics to be valued. Ability to listen and to communicate directly and clearly, both verbally and non-verbally, are important considerations, as is the maturity to be able to reveal problems when they occur and to ask for help and support. Comfortableness with physical contact with children is essential; there is nothing stronger than a hug, a silent holding or a pat on the back to convince children they are loved.

Following your week with the childminder you will be in a position to decide. Even when you have chosen a childminder, it is wise to maintain your observation when you take the children to and from the person. Ask the childminder for feedback on how things went for the day and watch for any discrepancies between what is said verbally and what her body is saying. Tone of voice, speed of speech, facial expression, body posture and level of eye contact are far more accurate barometers of how things really were than are verbal reassurances.

Be sure to communicate that this is a partnership-in-parenting arrangement and that you are there to help, advise and support in any way possible. It is frequently the case that a parent will not enquire, question or communicate concerns for fear of upsetting the childminder. The priority is your child's security, and once you communicate in a way that is respectful, open, direct and supportive, then possibilities of causing offence are eliminated. When childminders react defensively to such positive enquiries, they are showing their inner vulnerabilities – and this should be a source of concern for you.

Repeating, at a randomly selected time, that initial process of sharing and observing the caring would be a further means of guaranteeing a good choice of childminder.

Finally, fair pay for fair care is a necessary consideration.

❑ *Safeguarding students' rights in the school*

Within any one school students can experience mixed responses in terms of respect for and valuing of their rights. Some teachers can create excellent relationships with students, whereas others, due to their own vulnerabilities, can exert undue pressure on them, or be critical, sarcastic and threatening. Such an uncertain environment is good for neither the students nor the teachers themselves. Students deserve the predictability and consistency of being related to in ways that are respectful and positively firm. This is a two-way street – what teachers give out is likely to be what they get back. The behaviours of teachers that most upset students are:

- Being shouted at
- Being ordered to do things
- Not being called by first name
- Being labelled, for example 'stupid', 'lazy', 'a no good', 'weak', 'average', 'dull'
- Being publicly scolded or upbraided
- Being physically threatened, pushed or shoved
- Experiencing cynicism, sarcasm and 'put down' messages
- Being compared to another student
- Not being allowed to express own opinion
- Being laughed at
- Not being listened to
- Not being liked
- Not experiencing patience when work is difficult
- Not feeling understood

- Receiving unfair treatment
- Being punished for mistakes

Such experiences have the sad effect of turning children against teachers, learning and school. Very often students, particularly those who suffer greatly, fail to emerge out of the shadow of the violation of their rights and go through life carrying ideas of revenge and avoiding the challenge of learning.

The rights of students most likely to be either unrecognised or violated by teachers are:

- The right to respect
- The right to be seen and valued for one's unique self
- The right to be different
- The right to make mistakes and experience failure
- The right to be requested and not ordered to do things
- The right to be communicated with in direct and clear ways
- The right to be listened to
- The right to physical, emotional, intellectual and social safety
- The right to fairness

There are many structures that can be put in place to safeguard the rights of students in the school.

Structures to safeguard students' rights in the school

• Listing of clearly defined rights of students (see Chapter 5) on prominent display	• Start-of-year meeting of student committee
• Listing of clearly defined responsibilities of teachers and fellow students (see Chapter 6) on prominent display	• Regular meetings of student committee
	• Listing of clearly defined sanctions to safeguard students' rights
• Student committee	• Back-up support systems inside and outside of school
• Student handbook	• Structures common to both students and teachers

- Student committee

The school should provide the time and resources for students
to form their own formal student committee with a represen-
tative from each class year. The brief of the student committee
can embrace many aspects of school life – sports, drama,
educational tours, social activities, curriculum – but its primary
focus should be to ensure that the rights of students are being
upheld by both teachers and fellow students. Certainly the
committee needs to be concerned also about the preservation
of teachers' rights and must have a clear policy of non-collusion
with any neglect of teachers' legitimate needs by students.
The student committee needs to form policies that safeguard
students from bullying and needs to be vigilant for students
who are on the periphery of student life. The student committee and discipline committee (see Chapter 10) should work
closely together and have a mutual reporting relationship. A
similar relationship could exist with the parents' association.

A further useful role for the student committee would be to
organise surveys on such issues as students' needs, grievances,
bullying and school ethos. The findings of such studies could
be presented at assembly, to the discipline committee and to
the parents' association. It is imperative that the role of the
student committee is taken seriously by both teachers and
parents. What is even more important is that the student
committee takes itself and its responsibilities seriously.

The student committee could also be responsible for pub-
lishing a yearly student handbook.

- Student handbook

The student handbook offers all sorts of possibilities for
students to present how they view the school, the curriculum,
teachers, discipline, sports, the examination system, parents'
involvement in education and so on. In particular, it can serve
the very valuable function of presenting the rights of students
and the responsibilities that teachers and parents have in
relation to these rights. The sanctions that students may employ
can also be clearly presented. Of course, rights, responsibilities
and sanctions are always a two-way process, and it would be

important that the handbook acknowledges this and encourages students to accept this reality.

The handbook can address the two ways of behaving that cause most distress in social systems – bullying and passivity. Students need to find ways to empower the student who is passive and ways to help the perpetrators of bullying. Students have the opportunity to create their own caring and just culture within the school and can develop powerful means of sanctioning those who do not respect the rights of their fellow students. This is a source of legitimate power that few schools have employed in the development of a positive and caring school culture. Students always need acceptance and inclusion by their peers, and the sanction of not being allowed to participate in extracurricular and purely student activities can be a major deterrent against the abuse of the rights of fellow students. Once the student who has threatened the rights of peers (or teachers) has acknowledged and shown determination to respect those rights, then inclusion must be restored quickly.

A diary of student activities for the year could also be included in the handbook. Students could be encouraged to present articles on topics relevant to their lives.

In second-level schools, transition year students are in an ideal position to produce the student handbook. In primary school, the final year students could be the ones to do this job.

▪ Start-of-year meeting of student committee

Election of the student committee is best done at the end of the school year so that the committee can be at the helm immediately at the beginning of the new school year. On the first day back to school, time must be allocated for the initial meeting of the committee to take place so that the committee has credibility. The purpose of this first meeting is to set an agenda for the year and to consider the discipline system and the committee's response to it. Preparations for a presentation to the morning assembly can begin; ideally this would be within the first week. Any urgent business – for example, bullying – could also be discussed and policies could be initiated to deal with it.

■ Regular meetings of student committee

Regular meetings of the student committee must be time-tabled and included in the diary of events for the year. Minutes of meetings should be kept, typed up and circulated at the subsequent meeting. The primary safeguarding purposes of regular meetings are to provide opportunities for students who need support and championing to consult with the committee and to monitor teacher–student and student–student relationships. They also provide for continuing liaison with the discipline committee (see Chapter 10) and parents' association.

■ Sanctions to safeguard students' rights

Just as teachers need sanctions to vindicate their rights so too do students. This may be seen as too radical a step to be taken on board by some teachers. Whether or not teachers accept the notion, students can create a variety of sanctions that will provide for preservation of their rights. It is important that students remind themselves that the sanctions they employ in

Sanctions to safeguard students' rights in the school
• Make a positive and firm request to teacher to respect the student's violated right • Make a request for an apology • Leave classroom and go to sanction room • Request to talk to teacher at end of class period • Inform teacher that the breach of right will be reported to one of the following: (a) parent, (b) class tutor, (c) vice-principal, (d) principal, (e) student committee,	(f) discipline committee, (g) parents' association or (h) board of management • Put on report • Verbally consult with designated person • Send letter to one or more of the following: (a) parents' association, (b) board of management, (c) school inspector, (d) Department of Education or (e) solicitor • Refuse to return to the teacher's class • Enrol in another school

response to a teacher's violation of their rights are not opportunities for one-upmanship but a means of restoring a lost status. The sanctions must be used in such a way that the rights of teachers are not jeopardised. If the latter happens, abuses rather than sanctions are now being wielded and the initial violation escalates to mutual violation of rights.

These sanctions are suggestions to help the students, with the back-up of the school, to formulate effective means of safeguarding their rights. Students will do well to keep in mind that a sanction is only a sanction when it safeguards, and that what works in one situation and with a particular teacher may not work in all situations and with all teachers. The aim must be to keep looking until a way is found to reinstate the violated right and maintain its sanctity.

The proposed sanction of being 'put on report' is similar to that proposed for teachers in relation to undisciplined students (see Chapter 10). There is no reason why the student committee should not develop a report card system to evaluate teachers' behaviours in relation to students. The more a school's discipline system recognises the equality of teachers and students in terms of rights and responsibilities, the greater the likelihood of it being successful.

■ Back-up support systems inside and outside of school

The back-up systems available to students to endorse and safeguard their rights must be active in their support. The most important sources of support lie within the school system:

- School managers
- Board of management
- Principal and vice-principal
- Discipline committee
- Student committee
- Teaching staff
- Students
- School inspector

Other sources of support outside the school include:

- Parents
- Parents' association
- Childline
- Church
- Department of Education
- Legal profession

The student committee needs to find ways of opening communication lines with each of these sources of help. A Student Day would be an opportunity to create such links.

■ Structures common to both students and teachers

There are some structures that can be employed by both students and teachers to safeguard their rights. While these structures are dealt with at more length in Chapter 10, their particular relevance to safeguarding students' rights is outlined below.

- Morning assembly
- School handbook and classroom notice-boards
- Discipline committee
- Sanction room

↪ Morning assembly

The morning assembly is a forum for the principal to remind students of their rights and the structures that exist to ensure they are safeguarded. Most of all, the assembly provides the opportunity for the principal to voice the permission to students to report any incident that has jeopardised their safety in the classroom or school. Unless students are given very definite permission, it can be too threatening for them to report an incident to the relevant person or structure – be that to the class tutor, vice-principal, principal, student committee or discipline committee. The strength that lies in revealing violations of rights must be frequently stressed. The sanctions that students can utilise must also be outlined at assembly, and on some occasions, a member of the student committee could be invited to speak for the students on matters of rights, responsibilities and school discipline.

➲ School handbook and classroom notice-boards
The public display in the school handbook and classroom notice-boards of students' rights, and teachers' and peers' responsibilities in relation to these rights, also copper-fastens the rights of students. The safeguarding sanctions should be set out in both the handbook and the notice-board. It is important to remember that it is not only teachers and parents who violate students' rights; fellow students can make a young person's life absolutely miserable. For too long a deaf ear has been turned to this sad phenomenon. Students who abuse the right to safety of other students have to be responded to firmly and positively. No student should have to come to school on a daily basis and face victimisation, intimidation or actual bodily harm from a fellow student. The school must ensure that proper supervision exists within the school grounds, in classrooms and on the way to and from school. The student committee can also have a role as one of the watchguards of how students relate to one another. Members of the local community need to be encouraged to report any incidents that they may witness on the way to the school. Most of all, the victims of bullying need to be made aware that there is strength in reporting these experiences and that the school is determined to act on their behalf. No stone must be left unturned to make the world of students safe.

➲ Discipline committee
The discipline committee needs to be there as much for students as it is for teachers. Students must be informed of the times the committee is available to them for consultation. If a serious breach of a right has occurred, an emergency meeting should be possible.

➷ Sanction room

Just as a teacher can safeguard her rights by requesting a student to go to the sanction room, so too a student can employ the sanction room to remove himself from further abuse by a teacher. The student, in this case, needs to assert to the teacher who has broken his trust and has not apologised that 'I no longer feel safe in this classroom and I am going to the sanction room to continue my studies until this breach of my right has been resolved'. The student should then leave the classroom, report the circumstances to his class tutor and then retire to the safety of the sanction room. The student should not return to the classroom until he feels it is safe to do so. Typically students are afraid to confront the unacceptable behaviours of teachers for fear of victimisation. They fear, for example, that the teacher will not take any further interest in their education. However, should such a reaction occur, this is a further violation of the student's right to be educated and has to be responded to with further confrontation.

CHAPTER 9

Safeguarding Parents' Rights

□ *Parents' rights need safeguarding too!*
□ *Safeguarding parents' rights in the home*
- Sanctions to safeguard parents' rights
- Sanction room
- Community-based safeguards

□ *Safeguarding parents' rights in the school*
- School handbook
- Parent–teacher meetings
- Parents' association and parental representation
- Formal and informal home–school communication systems
- Sanctions to safeguard parents' rights
- Back-up support systems

□ *Parents' rights need safeguarding too!*

Parents are the architects of the family, but their architectural skills require considerable training, support and continuous updating in a quickly changing world. Teachers would do well to view parents as major allies in their role as educationalists. Parents have rights in relation to their children's education and in their relations with teachers: valuing, safeguarding and upholding those rights will go a long way towards strengthening that alliance. Many parents feel that teachers do not have regard for them and are considerably threatened by meetings with teachers. The parents' own experiences in school can militate against their feeling safe enough to form liaisons with teachers. The great need for parents and teachers to become a collective power for the development of children can no longer be ignored and the resolution of difficulties on both sides is paramount.

In the context of discipline, the rights that parents are more likely to complain are violated are:

By children:

- Right to respect
- Right to be seen for self
- Right to say 'no' to demands
- Right to physical safety
- Right to emotional, intellectual and social safety

By teachers:

- Right to respect
- Right to partnership in their children's education
- Right to be consulted when children are not coping in school
- Right to be communicated with in direct and clear ways

There are parents who are victimised by their own children and live under appalling threats of intimidation, violence and tirades of abuse. There are other parents who have been passive in asserting their own rights and have created children who are overdemanding and insensitive to the rights of others. Both sets of parents need to seek help to identify, assert and safeguard their rights.

❏ *Safeguarding parents' rights in the home*

When children control parents, safeguards have to be found to reinstate the parents' violated rights. The last thing parents need to hear is 'it's not my business' or 'you shouldn't have had kids if you don't know how to control them'. Parents do not deliberately invite neglect of their rights. However, factors such as their own personal vulnerability or poor marital relationship or the repetition of the failed parenting they experienced themselves as children are possible reasons why they have not learned to cope with their own parenting responsibilities. Structures are needed to safeguard their rights during the process of resolving their own personal and interpersonal difficulties. Where there is abuse of their physical right to safety by adolescent or young adult children, the safeguarding structures of legal protection orders or refuge centres are now available to besieged parents. However, there are few outside-the-home safeguards for parents whose emotional, intellectual or social safety is at risk from their children.

Structures to safeguard parents' rights in the home
<ul><li>Listing of clearly defined rights of parents (see Chapter 5) on prominent display</li><li>Listing of clearly defined responsibilities of children (see Chapter 6) on prominent display</li><li>Family handbook (see Chapter 8)</li><li>Regular family meetings (see Chapter 8)</li></ul> <ul><li>Listing of clearly defined sanctions to safeguard parents' rights</li><li>Sanction room</li><li>Community respite service from parenting</li><li>Community 'safe place'</li><li>Parenting advice and help centre</li><li>'Parentline', the telephone helpline for parents</li><li>Back-up support systems</li></ul>

Some of the structures proposed for parents are similar to those needed to safeguard the rights of children in the home. The difference is that parents must use these structures to express and safeguard their own rights. Not only must they assert their own rights and their children's responsibilities in relation to those rights, but they must also employ the family handbook, family meetings and sanctions to bring home the message of the sanctity of their rights. The most common pitfall for parents when safeguarding their rights is being unpredictable and inconsistent across different children and situations. From their earliest years, children need to see that no violation, no matter how small, will be ignored and also that their rights are held in the same high regard as those of their parents and each of their siblings.

■ Sanctions to safeguard parents' rights

In applying sanctions, parents would be wise to consider the two main dimensions of discipline. Firstly, they must take account of their own violated rights and only when safeguards have restored those rights do they consider the second dimension of enquiry, which is the reasons for their children's distressing behaviour. These two dimensions must be kept separate, as their enmeshment makes for ineffective safeguarding of rights. Naturally, parents must evaluate whether or not their behaviour may have transgressed children's rights and precipitated a like reaction on the part of their children. If this has occurred, the rights of both parties have been violated; both now need to take responsibility for their own violations and also ensure the safeguarding of their own rights. In the immediate situation the best safeguard for both parties to the conflict is space from one another.

Sanctions to safeguard parents' rights in the home

- Make a positive and firm request to stop the offensive behaviour
- Make a request for an apology
- Remove self from child's presence
- Confine child to room or house
- Deprive child of privileges (for example, pocket money, television viewing)
- Inform child that the breach of right will be reported to one of the following: (a) other parent or guardian, (b) aunt or uncle, (c) grandparent, (d) neighbour, (e) teacher, (f) family doctor or (g) police
- Report the breach to designated person
- Request child to go to sanction room
- In presence of child, ring Parentline or agency that provides help
- Leave house and go to neighbour for help
- Ring police

When applying sanctions, it is essential that parents resist the temptation to punish children for violating their rights. Punishing responses invariably violate the rights of children and aggravate an already difficult situation. Like parents and teachers, children do not engage in these actions to hurt parents. The sources may lie in low self-esteem, in experience of not feeling wanted or loved, or in hidden experiences of physical, emotional or sexual abuse. Of course, parents must resort immediately to actions that re-establish their rights; not to do so would be a neglect of themselves and poor modelling for their children. But they must ensure that their safeguarding responses do not jeopardise their children's rights. They need to let children know that the sanction is not employed to punish but to demonstrate the parents' seriousness about gaining respect for their rights.

One final point in the use of sanctions is that immediately the violated right has been reinstated, parents must then not harp on about the child's ill-disciplined conduct. If there is continued focus on the problematic behaviour, this puts the attention on the child who has violated the parents' rights but the purpose of sanctioning is to focus on re-establishing safety for the victims. Going beyond sanctioning is engaging in punishment and is no longer discipline. Furthermore, once the child has restored respect for the parents, for example by apologising and stopping the behaviours that threatened the parents' rights, then these desirable responses should be reinforced.

■ Sanction room

It is valuable to have a designated room in the home which can be employed as a sanction room. However, some children may continue to act out when sent to the sanction room and thereby continue to violate their parents' rights; parents now need to employ stronger safeguarding measures, for example telephone for outside help (neighbour, other parent, police) or leave the house.

■ Community-based safeguards

Some safeguards need to be community based. Parents need the support of other parents, very much in the same way that teachers need the support of each other, to manage their major responsibilities for children's well-being. There are some parents who can afford to pay for a relief parenting service. However, a well-organised group of parents could create a free rota system.

A safe place in the community for parents under threat from their children could be set up locally, or the church in the area could offer such a service. When the children are under sixteen years, an emergency parenting service could be sent in to monitor the situation in the home. It is regrettable that many parents do not seek help when needed, partly because of fear of judgment and partly because they do not want to expose their vulnerability. The more parents acknowledge that parenting demands enormous personal and interpersonal resources, the more they are likely to seek support from each other.

A locally based parenting advice and help centre is another structure needed to back up the rights of parents. Easy access and well-trained personnel are required to make this service effective.

Childline offers a major safeguarding service to children, and Parentline is a worthwhile complement. Refuge centres, social work services, the police and the family doctor are other possible sources of support. Addresses and phone numbers of these agencies could be put in the family handbook and on a strategically placed notice-board.

❏ *Safeguarding parents' rights in the school*

Parents need to create safeguards that uphold their rights regarding their children's education. At present, many parents feel threatened by teacher–parent meetings or by being asked to come to the school because of unacceptable behaviours on the part of their child. Parents may also be anxious about approaching a teacher with concerns about a child's academic progress or with complaints from their child of inappropriate behaviours on the part of a teacher or principal. There are many factors that may make it difficult for parents to approach teachers:

- Parents' own poor self-esteem
- Parents feeling like a child going to see the teacher
- Past unpleasant experiences with teachers when parents themselves were pupils
- Parents feeling inferior

- Fear of being judged or criticised
- Not knowing the teachers
- Teachers who appear unapproachable
- 'Superior' attitude on the part of teachers or principal
- Formality of meeting
- Parents feeling intimidated by a principal or teacher
- Lack of communication between school and home

There are a number of things that teachers and principals can do to reduce these restraining factors and to uphold the rights of parents:

- Be more approachable
- Introduce themselves by their first names
- Call parents by their first names
- Encourage parents to come to the school to talk about their children's educational development
- Organise social get-togethers
- Ask parents for help and advice
- Invite parents to participate in school development projects
- Be warm and friendly and not hide behind a professional mask
- Show obvious interest in and care for children
- Approach parents sensitively on their children's discipline problems
- Be accepting and affirming of parents

Whether or not teachers and principals make it easier for parents to establish their rights in relation to the school, parents themselves must be active in creating structures that safeguard their rights and be determined to implement these when their rights come under threat.

Structures to safeguard parents' rights in the school	
• Listing of clearly defined rights of parents (see Chapter 5) on prominent display • Listing of clearly defined responsibilities of teachers (see Chapter 6) on prominent display • School handbook • Regular parent–teacher meetings • Parents' association	• Parent representatives on board of management • Parent representatives on discipline committee • Formal home–school communication system • Informal home–school communication system • Listing of clearly defined sanctions to safeguard parents' rights • Back-up support systems

■ School handbook

A section of the school handbook should be given over to defining the role of parents in the school and listing their rights and the school's responsibilities in relation to those rights. A diary of parental activities for the forthcoming year could also be included. The parents' association could take responsibility for preparing this material.

■ Parent–teacher meetings

The start-of-year parent–teacher meeting is an opportunity for parents to voice not only their rights but also their interest in being involved with the school. However, parents may need to insist on more meetings to ensure continued awareness of their rights and the provision of a forum to voice any dissatisfactions.

■ Parents' association and parental representation

The parents' association is a major force to safeguard parents' rights. It must be an independent body and not in any way be subservient to the principal or school manager. It needs to meet regularly and all parents need to be made aware of how the association can be contacted and how it can act on their behalf. There needs to be a three-way reporting relationship between the discipline committee (see Chapter 10), the board of management and the parents' association. It is important that each body cooperates with the others in the maintenance and vindication of the rights of parents, students and teachers. Parental involvement with the board of management and the discipline committee further safeguards parents' rights.

- Formal and informal home–school communication systems

Parents and teachers need to agree both formal and informal communication systems that operate for the good of both of them. All parents need to be informed and encouraged to avail of these resources.

- Sanctions to safeguard parents' rights

Sanctions are always a final resort in the safeguarding of rights, and parents, like teachers and students, have every right to make use of them when their rights are under threat.

Sanctions to safeguard parents' rights in the school	
• Make a positive and firm request for meeting with teacher or principal • Meet with teacher or principal • Verbally inform teacher or principal that the breach of right will be reported to one or more of the following: (a) principal, (b) school manager, (c) board of management, (d) school inspector, (e) parents' association, (f) Department of Education or (g) solicitor	• Inform teacher or principal in writing that the breach of right will be reported to one or more of the people or bodies designated • Report the breach of right as warned • Remove child temporarily from school • Enrol child in another school • Report the breach of right to media

It is imperative that parents use sanctions only to the point of re-establishing their rights. Sanctions are not there to embarrass the school or any teacher. Parents who pursue this latter line are not likely to be successful in vindicating their rights. Clearly, when parents are compelled to consider using the sanctions of either removing their children from the school or enrolling them elsewhere, they must consider the needs and the opinions of the children. Some parents can go on a crusade and forget that their children have rights and needs too.

■ Back-up support systems

The final safeguarding measure open to parents is back-up support in the form of community action groups and legal and social bodies that safeguard parents' rights in relation to their children's education. The Irish constitution enshrines the rights of parents as primary educators of their children. Voluntary bodies such as the Irish Society for the Prevention of Cruelty to Children will also back up the rights of parents. Parentline is yet another source of support.

CHAPTER 10

Safeguarding Teachers' Rights

❑ *Teachers' rights need safeguarding too!*
- Sanctions to safeguard teachers' rights
- Sanction room
- Annual school handbook
- Start-of-year teachers' meeting on discipline
- Start-of-year parent–teacher meeting
- Constructive use of daily assembly of students and teachers
- Discipline committee
- Frequent staff meetings on discipline
- Use of classroom notice-boards
- Recourse to parents
- Back-up support systems

❑ *Teachers' rights need safeguarding too!*

Too many of the rights of teachers have been neglected and it is this that underlies the highly stressful nature of teaching and the rising tide of discipline problems. Clearly, the level of neglect differs from school to school, and it is the responsibility of teachers within the unique culture of their own school to identify and express unmet needs and to demand structures that safeguard their rights.

From my own experience as a teacher and from feedback through working with teachers, the rights of teachers most likely to be neglected are:

- The right to respect
- The right to teach
- The right to order and attention
- The right to a positive response to reasonable requests
- The right to direct and clear communication from students, colleagues and principals

126

- The right to physical and emotional safety
- The right to be consulted by principals on matters that pertain to teachers' responsibilities
- The right to be listened to

It is necessary that teachers themselves become sufficiently empowered to own and express these rights. But when rights are not honoured, teachers need to have resort to structures that safeguard their unmet rights. If such structures have not been created, teachers must demand that they be established as a matter of urgency.

The structures that schools invent to safeguard teachers' rights need to be geared clearly to upholding the rights of teachers and must not in any way threaten the rights of students and parents.

Structures to safeguard teachers' rights	
<ul><li>Listing of clearly defined rights of teachers (see Chapter 5) on prominent display</li><li>Listing of clearly defined responsibilities of students, fellow teachers and managers (see Chapter 6) on prominent display</li><li>Listing of clearly defined sanctions to safeguard teachers' rights</li><li>Sanction room</li><li>Annual school handbook that has a major section on discipline</li><li>Start-of-year teachers' meeting on discipline</li></ul>	<ul><li>Start-of-year parent–teacher meeting</li><li>Constructive use of daily assembly of students and staff</li><li>Discipline committee</li><li>Frequent staff meetings on discipline</li><li>Use of classroom notice-boards for declarations of teachers' rights, students' responsibilities and sanctions</li><li>System for recourse to parents when students are not being responsible</li><li>Back-up support systems inside and outside the school</li></ul>

Principals or teachers who balk at the list of actions needed to safeguard teachers' rights need to reconsider their commitment to creating an effective discipline system and are hardly in a position to complain if they encounter neglect of their rights. When you value and own your own rights and see that it is your responsibility to uphold them, you will be more likely to commit yourself to the structures that safeguard your rights.

■ Sanctions to safeguard teachers' rights

Sanctions are a potent structure for the safeguarding of teachers' rights. Their sole purpose must be to safeguard and they must not be viewed in the traditional way as a punishment for misbehaviour. The traditional view of sanctions as punishment passes the responsibility for teachers' rights onto students, assumes that students' misconduct is aimed deliberately at teachers and misses the emotional intelligence of the difficult behaviours (see Chapter 4). A blaming attitude serves only to create more distance in the relationships between teachers and students. The focus of the sanction must stay on the teacher whose rights have been violated, and the mistake must not be made of making the student the focus.

Sanctions must spring from the teacher's determination to reinstate and safeguard the blocked right. The purpose is not to get back at the student. Clearly, then, sanctions such as the doing of endless lines or extra schoolwork do not in any way convey the appropriate message that neither the school nor the individual teacher will tolerate any violation of a teacher's right. The sanction needs to ensure that the rights of the teacher will not be further contravened. For example, if a teacher in a respectful way makes a request of a student and is met with a 'fuck off' response, the first sanction to be applied would be a verbal one: 'John, I'm not accepting such language from you and I would like you to show respect by apologising for what you've said'. If no apology is forthcoming, the teacher would then introduce a second sanction by, firstly, reminding John that she the teacher has the right to be communicated with in a respectful way and, secondly, requesting him to leave the room and go to the sanction room. If the student refuses to leave the room, the teacher then requests one of the other students to ask the vice-principal to come to the classroom (third sanction). The whole aim of this process is the strong assertion by the teacher that she has too much respect for herself to ignore the abuse of her right to be respected by the students. This process will need to continue until the teacher is guaranteed emotional and social safety. Otherwise she should not receive the student back into her classroom.

Many teachers and parents might view such actions on the part of the teacher as going too far, but letting go of a relatively minor misdemeanour can quickly lead to the occurrence of major violations of teachers' rights. Furthermore, in this sequence of actions there is no desire to punish the student, but there certainly is a determination to uphold the right of the teacher. If the student had responded positively to any of the proposed sanctions, the issue would have been resolved.

The implementation of a sanction must be carried out in such a way that the student knows precisely what right of the teacher has been transgressed by his behaviour and what is required of him so that there is no further abuse of a right. The student now has a choice: if he chooses to respect the teacher's rights, the matter is resolved; if he chooses to continue the neglect of the teacher's rights, he invites the consequences of that behaviour – the safeguarding sanction.

There are certain guidelines in the use of sanctions as a safeguard:

1. It needs to be made clear to students that *sanctions exist not just for their transgressions but also for the transgressions of teachers and parents.* Parents and teachers may find this concept difficult, but children sense injustice and are quick to recognise double standards of behaviour.

2. When possible, *sanctions should be the natural result of the irresponsible behaviour.* For example, if a student disrupts classwork and thereby violates the right of the teacher to teach and the other students to learn, then a natural sanction is to deprive him of break time and, if he persists, to request him to go to the sanction room. If a student in temper throws materials all over the classroom, thereby not respecting property, a natural sanction is to give him the task of tidying up the room.

3. *Sanctions must be predictable and consistent.* Predictability means that the student (and teacher and parents) is aware of rights and responsibilities and knows that any violation of the rights of others will inevitably lead to the application of an appropriate safeguarding sanction. Consistency means that no matter which teacher may be involved or which student is blocking the rights of others, the same sanction will be applied.

4. *Sanctions must be fair.* The sanction must only go as far as is necessary to reinstate and safeguard the right that has been violated. When sanctions are agreed by the whole staff or a school discipline committee and not left to the whim of a particular teacher, then the possibility of unfairness is considerably lessened. Frequent reviews of the discipline system also guard against injustice.

5. *Sanctions must be objective.* This means that they arise clearly from some legitimate right of the teacher and their function is to vindicate that right. It is vital that the teacher holds onto her ownership of her right and the action she is taking to reassert that right. If she blames the student, objectivity is lost and the student is reinforced in his undisciplined conduct.

6. *Sanctions must emphasise the rights of the teacher and the responsibilities of the student in terms of respecting that right.* Students need to be reminded that these expectations are a two-way process.

7. If possible, *sanctions should be withheld until the teacher understands the 'cry for help' underlying the student's unacceptable behaviour.* The teacher can then assign the sanction in a manner which clearly demonstrates that understanding; for example, 'John, I am aware you dislike this subject but I cannot allow you to disrupt my teaching and I am requesting you to stop that behaviour'. Sometimes it may not be obvious why a student is engaging in ill-disciplined actions, but nevertheless order needs to be restored immediately. In that case the sanction should be applied with an additional follow-up: 'John I'd like to talk to you later about why you are choosing to act in this way'.

8. *Sanctions must be applied in a way that the student does not become fearful of the teacher.* Fear is an unfair weapon for adults to employ in their interactions with children. Its presence means that a fundamental right of the student to feel physically and emotionally safe in the classroom is being violated. Two wrongs never make a right. Furthermore, the student who is frightened may agree to anything, but when he recovers he will have learned nothing and his next act of ill-discipline may be worse than the first.

9. *Sanctions must never involve the assignment of 'lines' or extra schoolwork or homework.* Such sanctions serve no purpose; they are seen by students as 'stupid' or 'unfair' and express absolutely nothing about the real function of a sanction, which is to safeguard rights.

10. *Students should be addressed by their first names when a sanction is being assigned.*

11. *Sanctions are more effectively applied when the teacher employs an 'I' rather than a 'you' message.* In the 'I' message, the teacher takes full ownership of the violated right; for example, 'Mary, I would like to be able to teach in an atmosphere of order and attention and will not accept your talking out of turn in class'. A 'you' communication – for example, 'Mary, you better stay quiet in my class or you'll be put on report' – is blaming in nature and generally creates more problems.

The list of sanctions below is meant to be indicative rather than exhaustive; the unique culture of the school and the age and number of the students will determine precisely which sanctions are appropriate.

Sanctions to safeguard teachers' rights	
• Positive and firm request for respect of teacher's rights • Request for an apology • Request of student to sit in another part of the classroom • Request of student to meet teacher at end of class • Student sent to sanction room with a meaningful purpose (this needs to be supervised and the supervisor needs clear directions on what academic task – for example, completion of classwork and homework not done – has been assigned to the student) • Deprivation of privileges (the possible withdrawal of an activity that a student enjoys can be a strong incentive to respect teachers' rights) • Warning of being sent to (a) class tutor (peculiar to second-level schools),	(b) vice-principal or (c) principal • Being put on report (many schools now employ a report card system which teachers are required to mark at the end of each class) • Being sent to (a) class tutor, (b) vice-principal or (c) principal • Arrangement made to meet discipline committee • Letter to parents • Meeting with parents (it is advisable when there are two parents to insist that both attend) • Written warning of suspension given to student and sent to parents • Suspension • Expulsion (this is the ultimate safeguard where the rights of teachers or other students are seriously under threat from a student)

■ Sanction room

A sanction room in a school is vital to the upholding of the rights of all. Its purpose is to have a safe place to request a student who has violated the rights of another to go to, so that the rights of the offended person are quickly reinstated. It also makes it more likely that the rights of the perpetrator will not come under threat by the reactions of others to his offensive behaviour. The room is not to be employed as a means of punishment or humiliation but as a vindication of rights. The room should be comfortable, with a couple of desks and chairs, and be situated so that a secretary, volunteer parent or principal can observe easily what is happening within.

■ Annual school handbook

An annual school handbook is an ideal means for a school to publicise its mission and the means whereby the aspirations contained in the mission statement will be upheld. The mission declaration needs to contain aims and objectives that focus on the welfare of teachers, students and parents.

Sample mission statement

This school is committed to upholding the legitimate rights of students, teachers and parents. Any violation of rights will be viewed seriously. The school's aim in the event of a violation of rights is to support the victim and reinstate the violated right, and the school is also concerned to help the perpetrator of socially unacceptable behaviours.

The staff of this school want to create a climate of physical, emotional, social and intellectual safety for students, teachers and parents so that teaching and learning can occur within relationships of mutual valuing and respect. With this in mind, the teachers of the school see education not just as providing students with knowledge and skills but also as providing for the emotional, social, sexual, physical and spiritual development of students. In this school we want students to be self-motivated and to be at peace with themselves, others and the world. Achievement of these aspirations by the school requires the help and cooperation of students, teachers and parents.

This mission statement is but one example of countless possibilities but its essence and its spirit should be contained in any formulation. It is recommended that the mission statement grows from the unique culture of the school so that it captures the needs of all those who cross the school's threshold.

Following the mission statement, the handbook should outline the rights and responsibilities of teachers, students and parents (see Chapters 5 and 6) and the sanctions that will be put in place for the perpetrators of any violation of rights, whether teachers, students or parents. The handbook could also include the school's aspirations on empowerment of its members and the means it employs to do this (see Chapter 7). The section on discipline in the handbook could finish with inviting the commitment and cooperation of all for the creation of a safe physical and emotional school environment so that teachers can teach and children can learn in mutual respect and celebration of each other.

It is best that parents receive a copy of this handbook prior to the first parent–teacher meeting at the start of the school year. A covering letter should accompany the handbook requesting parents to read it carefully so that any difficulties with any of its contents can be presented at the meeting.

■ Start-of-year teachers' meeting on discipline

A meeting of teachers to discuss discipline should be held prior to the start-of-year parent–teacher meeting and prior to receiving students into the school. The meeting, which should be of at least two hours' duration, must have no item on the agenda other than discipline. This meeting needs to address any particular difficulties individual teachers may be having with discipline; however, unless a non-judgmental and safe environment is created, teachers will not reveal their problems in classroom management.

The sections in the school handbook on the school's mission and discipline procedures should be discussed. The formation of discipline strategies would already have been done in consultation with the teachers and the purpose of the meeting would be to ratify the proposals. The principal has a key role to play here in emphasising that cohesiveness among staff and consistency and predictability in applying the discipline procedures are essential to the effectiveness of the discipline system. She needs to encourage teachers to voice any reservations they might have and to stress that the system proposed is not 'cast in stone' and may need modification. The principal also needs to voice her determination that no teacher should undergo continued exposure to ill-disciplined conduct on the part of students. She needs to add also that no student must suffer distressing behaviour on the part of a teacher. The climate she should aim to create is one where student–teacher relationships are valuing and affirming and where teachers let students know in firm and positive ways that they will not accept any violation of their legitimate rights.

The principal also needs to reassure teachers that she will back up fair responses to violations of their rights. Discussion needs also to be engendered on how perpetrators, particularly persistent ones, can be given the help they need to take on the responsibilities entailed in being a student of the school. Once again, it would be wise to confirm that teachers' rights will be safeguarded during the time it takes to help students with discipline problems. The principal must emphasise that teachers will not have to face into daily disruption in their classes.

In this meeting the rights of teachers and the consequent responsibilities of students, colleagues and managers must be restated. It would be wise to follow this with a discussion on the proposed sanctions for violation of teachers' rights and how these sanctions might best be applied.

■ Start-of-year parent–teacher meeting

The start-of-year parent–teacher meeting is more productive when it is held prior to intake of students into the school. Parents have a responsibility to share with the school the educational development of their children. Given that responsibility and the present drive towards partnership between teachers and parents, attendance at this meeting needs to be obligatory. Teachers need the back-up of parents if they are to be effective in teaching children, let alone resolving difficult behaviours. Where there are two parents (or other adult with a major role in the parenting of children), both should be invited to attend the meeting. Students should not be accepted into the new school year until some form of meaningful contact has been had with the parents; to do otherwise is to collude with parental non-participation in education. Experience shows that the students who present the most difficulties in school come from homes where parents are not managing to parent effectively. At least when these parents come to the school there is a greater chance to help their children. It is of paramount importance that parents feel it is both socially and emotionally safe for them to come to the school. They need to feel that their presence and input matter and to recognise that it is through their support and cooperation that teachers can do their best for all aspects of their children's welfare.

One purpose of the meeting is to acquaint the parents with the ethos of the school as well as to outline the range of school and extra-school activities. It also offers an opportunity for the parents and teachers to get to know one another. It is important that the meeting addresses the long-term nature of the relationship between parents and teachers.

One of the primary purposes of the meeting is to address the issue of school discipline and parents' role in its operation. Even though parents should have received a copy of the school handbook prior to the meeting, it would be unwise to assume they have read it thoroughly, or even at all. The principal needs to explain the safeguarding nature of the discipline system of the school and to stress that the system is there not just for the students but also for teachers and parents. The rights and accompanying mutual responsibilities of students, teachers and parents need to be clearly illustrated, along with the sanctions that are designed to safeguard violated rights. It needs to be firmly stated that the school is determined to vindicate the rights of all, and that the school is concerned to help the perpetrator (whether student, teacher or parent) of ill-disciplined conduct, but never at the expense of the victim. It must be seen that the vindication of victims' rights is a separate issue from helping perpetrators of ill-disciplined behaviour, because it is the confusion of both of these issues that in the past made the resolution of discipline problems difficult. The principal needs to be clear that it is the responsibility of all three groups – parents, teachers and students – to cooperate and to support the fair discipline system being proposed. An opportunity to clarify issues must be given to parents.

The meeting also offers an opportunity to encourage parents to take a more active role in the school and to use whatever facilities are being provided. All the evidence suggests that the greater the level of interaction between parents and teachers, the greater the level of support and cooperation. Both parents and teachers need all the support they can get for the two most difficult professions of all – parenting and teaching.

If not included in the school handbook, a programme of the school's activities for the year, including the dates and times of parent–teacher meetings, should be made available towards the end of the meeting.

- Constructive use of daily assembly of students and teachers

The daily assembly is an ideal forum for reminders to the students (and teachers) on how they need to behave in relation to one another, teachers, property and schoolwork. It must be stressed that the discipline system is there for both students and teachers and that the students' parents have a vital role to play. The whole aim of the discipline system is to make it physically, emotionally, intellectually, creatively and socially safe for everybody to be in school and to come to the school. The principal must make no bones about how strongly the rights of both students and teachers will be vindicated in the face of violations and must emphasise that whilst the staff are deeply concerned to help any student who is experiencing any difficulty (for example, bullying, learning difficulties, unfair treatment by teachers, unhappy home situation, sexual abuse), the school cannot allow those difficulties to block the rights of others.

Students could be informed at assembly of the rights and responsibilities of students, teachers and parents and the sanctions that follow violation of these rights. Provision of lists of these would reinforce understanding of the discipline system. Students could also be informed about the discipline committee and the representation of students on that committee.

During the first week of the school year these messages should be repeated daily at the morning assembly. Thereafter, at least one major reference to the discipline system and ethos of the school should be made on a weekly basis.

At all meetings the need for the support and cooperation of students must be voiced, and when these responses are given they should be reinforced.

▪ Discipline committee

Most schools have boards of management whose members include school managers, principal, vice-principal and parents. This is an important body as it means that decision-making is not left in the hands of one person, such as the principal. A reporting relationship needs to exist between the discipline committee and the board of management, particularly in situations where either a victim or perpetrator of under-controlled behaviour is highly at risk. For example, victims of bullying have been known to either commit suicide or murder the perpetrator.

At second level, the discipline committee could include the vice-principal, two other staff members, two senior students and, when possible, one or two parents. In primary schools, instead of two students, two parents who are available during school times could be invited on to the committee. What is needed is a fair representation of all the groups concerned.

The discipline committee's main responsibility is to monitor and frequently review the operation of the school's discipline system. A further important function is to arbitrate on the 'grey' areas of what a particular responsibility or sanction means. Rights and responsibilities may mean different things to different teachers, students and parents. Also, students and teachers who are in conflict may present different versions of a violation of a right. It is the difficult task of the committee to get to the real story so that fairness and justice operate. The decisions of this committee must not be overruled by any one teacher or by the principal. There can be a procedure that allows appeal to the board of management, but during appeal it is imperative that the rights of both victim and perpetrator are safeguarded.

The committee needs to have set school times when it is available for consultation. These times can also serve the function of supporting both teachers and students in the implementation of the discipline system. The discipline committee needs to be particularly sensitive to teachers or students who are not coping with discipline and who may need personal empowerment and peer support to assert and actively safeguard their rights. In some cases outside professional help may be required and this needs to be discreetly handled.

The operation of the discipline committee must not be seen as an extracurricular activity but as part and parcel of the everyday life of the school. Only in this way will a school demonstrate its commitment to effective discipline and to the welfare of all.

■ Frequent staff meetings on discipline

A frequent complaint of teachers is the infrequency of staff meetings, and even more so the few, if any, meetings that are arranged to discuss discipline. Teaching and learning thrive in an environment of order, safety, friendliness and fairness. This atmosphere does not happen by chance, but on the contrary needs considerable input to bring it about. When discipline is perceived in the broad context outlined in this book, the necessity of frequent meetings on discipline (with no other item on the agenda) becomes very evident. The discipline committee could present a report at the beginning of each of these staff discipline meetings. The principal must then facilitate the airing of any difficulties particular staff members may be experiencing and attempt, with the support of the rest of the staff, to resolve them.

Confrontation may be necessary for those teachers who are not operating the system effectively. This needs to be done in a way that is non-critical, but which nevertheless acknowledges that such non-cooperation weakens the discipline system and jeopardises the rights of colleagues. The meetings may need to look particularly at those students (or indeed teachers) who are reluctant to take on their responsibilities, and decisions may have to be made on how others can be protected from their lack of care. This is a difficult issue but one that cannot be ignored.

The rights of the principal and other staff members and students cannot be sacrificed because one or two teachers are not cooperating, no matter what the source of their non-compliance. Certainly, help must be made available to these teachers, but structures are needed to prevent them from perpetrating behaviours that block the rights of others. One such structure is private consultation between the teacher and the principal. A second structure could involve the school inspector. A third structure could be to seek a decision from the board of management. The Department of Education should also make provision for safeguarding teachers and students from such a teacher. When such structures do not exist, the teacher herself, her colleagues, school management, the students, the parents and the school are all seriously let down by the educational system. Confrontation is always an act of caring; absence of safeguarding structures is an act of neglect.

Finally, if it is acceptable that a student can be sent to the sanction room or suspended or expelled because of a serious threat to others, why cannot similar consequences exist for teachers?

■ Use of classroom notice-boards

The rights and the responsibilities of students, teachers and parents and the safeguarding sanctions could usefully be posted on notice-boards in each classroom so that neither teachers nor students can claim ignorance of them. Their posting means too that they can be readily referred to in a situation of conflict. Most of all, the posting of rights, responsibilities and sanctions acts as a reminder to all of the sanctity of their rights and the school's commitment to upholding them.

■ Recourse to parents

A system needs to be in place that allows consultation with parents when a student is not responding to discipline expectations, despite repeated sanctions. This system should be agreed with parents at the start-of-year meeting. The medium of contact can be phone, letter, visit to the parents by the student's class tutor, school liaison officer, principal or vice-principal, or visit of parents to the school. The tone of the contact must be that the parents' help and support are needed by the school so that some agreed course of action can be put in place to help their troubled child get back on a welfare path again. It needs to be made abundantly clear to the parents that their child cannot continue to attend class unless there is clear evidence that there will be no recurrence of the abuse of others' rights. It could also be pointed out that the child cannot thrive educationally until the sources of his non-compliance are detected and healed. Many principals resist the notion of barring a child from the classroom even though the learning of others is being disrupted, on the grounds that the child cannot learn if he is not in the classroom. But it must be seen that the child's mere presence in the classroom does not in any way guarantee learning, and indeed the focus of such a troubled child is likely to be very far away from learning.

If parents resist these discipline steps, the rights of teachers and other students must continue to be upheld and the school must insist that the parents accept their responsibility in the matter before further progress can be made. By adopting this approach, the school is truly showing care for the student. If parents continue to resist, then recourse to a social worker may be necessary to get the help the child needs. It is important that either a school counsellor or a teacher to whom the child relates well keeps the student abreast of attempts to help him. Even if he is on ongoing detention in the sanction room or is under suspension, contact must be maintained. Even when the ultimate sanction of expulsion is imposed, continued caring contact by the school will not go amiss.

■ Back-up support systems

Generally speaking, teachers have not felt supported in vindicating their rights. However, they are partly responsible for this themselves as they have been largely passive in the vindication of their rights. They complain, and not without justice, that the focus is primarily on the student and the curriculum and that their needs do not seem to matter. The more support systems teachers have, the greater the likelihood of effective schools. The most important source of support for teachers is their own colleagues and the principal and vice-principal.

These sources of support can sometimes be there on an informal level, but formal systems are much more tangible and available. Certainly, staff meetings are an ideal forum for support to be expressed. Both the principal and vice-principal need to be available and approachable; the times of availability need to be clearly specified and, of course, they must always be available in times of crisis.

Teachers' centres, teachers' unions, the school inspectorate, boards of management and parents' associations are systems outside the school that teachers, when threatened, can avail of for support.

PART IV

Prevention and Intervention

CHAPTER 11

All Discipline Starts with Self

☐ *Rights in relationship with self*
☐ *Self-responsibility*
☐ *Personal structures to safeguard rights*
☐ *Self-control*

    ■ Early identification of emergency feelings
    ■ Emergency feelings are a message about self
    ■ Action on emergency feelings

☐ *Rights in relationship with self*

The person most likely to violate your rights is yourself. For example, when you are angry with yourself, or you label yourself as a 'fool' or 'stupid', or you push yourself when tired, or you miss meals, eat on the run or drive dangerously, or you ridicule yourself, you are no longer creating a safe physical, emotional, social and intellectual world for yourself. And you are hardly in a strong position to request others to respect your rights when you neglect yourself so much. Conversely, when you do not tolerate violations of your rights by others, you practise good care of self. Moreover, personal neglect commonly leads to interpersonal neglect. And again, the opposite observation is true: when you value and uphold your own rights, you are more likely to be similarly caring of the rights of others.

Adults need to be aware not only of their rights in relationships with others, but also of their rights in their relationship with themselves. Children, too, need to be educated about rights, responsibilities and safeguarding strategies in their relationships with themselves. Of course, awareness in itself is not sufficient but needs to be backed up by personal responsibility and safeguarding mechanisms to ensure maintenance of rights. The rights you have in relationship with self are not dissimilar to those in relationship with others:

- I have the right to love myself.
- I have the right to respect and accept my unique self.
- I have the right to listen to myself.
- I have the right to communicate with myself in a respectful way.
- I have the right to fail and the right to succeed.
- I have the right to nurture myself.
- I have the right to my own beliefs.
- I have the right to treat myself fairly and justly.
- I have the right to be independent and self-reliant.
- I have the right to believe in my vast potential.

It is quite extraordinary the number of people who have no sense of their right to love, respect, nurture and take care of themselves. These deficits in self-care arise from a culture that reared children to live their lives for others and punished them for being there for themselves. You could love your neighbour but you dare not love yourself! Not only is this philosophy contrary to the Christian message 'love God with all your heart and your neighbour as yourself'; it also runs contrary to the findings of psychoanalysis and psychotherapy that the relationship with self is the basis of healthy relationships with all others. The suggestion that love of self is vainglorious and selfish was a clever manipulation to maintain control of people. The person who loves self does not tolerate control, domination or abuse by others. Those who accept self are in a better position to be unselfish and they not only respect themselves but respect and value others, are fair and are strong advocates of the rights of others. Those who hate or dislike self are highly dependent on others, leading them to be aggressive, dominant and controlling, or passive, fearful and timid or possessive, inflexible and intolerant.

Parents and teachers need to give themselves permission to have a warm, accepting and loving relationship with themselves, not only for the sake of their own emotional, social, intellectual and physical well-being, but also for the sake of the healthy development of their children and their students. It is primarily through witnessing adults' relationships with themselves that children learn to love, accept, value and nurture themselves.

The rights to be independent, be self-reliant, have your own beliefs, live your own life and assert your own vast intellectual potential are rights that many adults are nervous of expressing, for fear of criticism, rejection or ridicule. Western culture has not been forceful in advocating the individuality of people, but instead it has tended to foster conformity, dependence and sameness. This is regrettable, as the powerhouse of creativity and productivity lies in each person acting out from his uniqueness and limitless potential. The more that home, school, community and state emphasise and affirm people's unique identities and believe in their vast capacity, the safer it will be for individuals to act on the relationship with themselves that is so crucial for them.

❏ *Self-responsibility*

As with your rights in relationship with others, your rights in relationship with yourself only have meaning when you take responsible action for them. This is a responsibility that many adults avoid, clinging protectively to 'passing the buck' for their welfare onto others. But each adult is responsible for meeting his personal rights and needs. When you take on this responsibility, you have the strength of self-reliance and independence of others; but when you lack a responsible relationship with self, you put yourself at the mercy of others.

A range of actions, or responsibilities, is required to uphold your rights in relationship with yourself:

- Physically care for self
- Develop a balanced lifestyle
- Listen to self
- Affirm frequently your worth, value, vast capability and uniqueness
- Identify, value and act on feelings
- Identify and take responsibility for your own emotional, sexual, intellectual and spiritual needs
- Spend time being with self

- Treat yourself fairly and justly
- Form and respect your own beliefs
- Encourage and praise your efforts at self-care
- Talk kindly and encouragingly to self
- Be supportive of self
- Challenge self

The responsibilities towards self that are least practised are 'being with self' and 'challenging self'. The ability to enjoy your own company is a strong index of maturity, as is the determination to continue to challenge yourself to progress further down the road of self-possession and spirituality.

❑ *Personal structures to safeguard rights*

A high regard for self makes it more likely you will responsibly commit yourself to owning and fulfilling your own needs and rights. You are certainly less likely to allow yourself to be blocked by the immaturity of others. However, because there are few of us who have reached the peaks of self-regard and self-responsibility, some personal structures are required to guard against violations of your rights by yourself:

- Having lists of personal rights and responsibilities
- Having a designated safe place
- Reading a declaration of self-esteem
- Reading or listening for personal development
- Having sanctions for yourself
- Time-management of rights and needs

You are much more likely to uphold personal rights when you have lists of personal rights and responsibilities which you read on a daily basis. If you have violated a self-right, a rereading of these lists may be sufficient to restore the neglected right. Similarly, if you have designated a safe place for yourself (for example, a particular room, church or scenic spot) where strong associations of self-regard, serenity and self-care are present, then an immediate retreat to this sanctuary will help restore equilibrium when a right is violated.

Reciting declarations of or listening to a tape on self-esteem following irresponsible care for self is another means of restoring your relationship with yourself. Similarly, reading a book or listening to a tape on personal development can help the process of reinstating a violated right.

When you sanction yourself, be sure to do so only to the point of the re-establishment of the violated right, since to go beyond that point is an act of punishment. When you fail to uphold a right, the natural sanction is to restore that right as quickly as possible. For example, when you berate and negatively label self, the natural sanction is to talk kindly and positively to yourself. Similarly when you miss meals, eat on the run, miss sleep or rush and race, the sanctions of doing precisely the opposite of those neglectful actions will immediately reinstate the abused rights. Sometimes, when the neglect of self has been serious and prolonged, stronger sanctions may be required to ensure a return to self-care, such as report neglect to your partner or a friend; go to a psychologist, counsellor or family doctor; or attend a health farm or health clinic.

Time-management is a good discipline for those who are neglectful of self. It ensures time and space for meeting threatened personal rights and needs and it quickly shows up recurring neglect. The idea is to plan your day so as to ensure that specific times and places are allocated to at-risk needs (for example, time for self, time for commuting between tasks to be done, time for meals, time for rest). It reinforces the process when you tick off completed assignments.

❏ *Self-control*

It is very important that parents and teachers do not make children, partners or colleagues bear the brunt of their own poor relationship with themselves. Such behaviour reflects lack of self-control and an attempt to make others responsible for your personal welfare. You have a right to make requests with regard to your interpersonal rights and needs. However, your personal care of yourself is entirely your own responsibility, unless you are sick or incapacitated.

Self-control involves learning and employing the actions needed to maintain responsibility for the meeting of your rights. Loss of control arises from attempting to blame either others or self for violations of your personal rights. Neither response results in positive action being taken to reinstate violated rights. Feelings are an important barometer of threats to rights, and self-control here involves a number of clear-cut responses:

- Early identification of emergency feelings
- The perception that emergency feelings are a message about self, not the other person
- Action on emergency feelings to the point of the reinstatement of a feeling of welfare

▪ Early identification of emergency feelings

Emergency feelings are those feelings that alert you to the existence of some real or imagined threat to your well-being, for example fear, sadness, anger, rage, depression, resentment, bitterness and fatigue. Women are far more literate than men when it comes to identifying emergency feelings except anger or rage. Men tend to be poor at recognising and acknowledging emergency feelings and can be at break-point before they realise what is happening emotionally to them. At this stage it is often too late, and they can lose self-control and dump their fear, vulnerability, anger, depression or bitterness on others.

Your body is a useful barometer of what may be happening to you emotionally. For example, fear can be physically experienced as a pain in your stomach or an increase in heart rate or pulse rate. Depression may express itself in loss of appetite, insomnia or an empty feeling in the stomach. Anger may present itself in a tightening-up of your whole body. Bitterness and resentment may emerge as a pain in the forehead, tightening of the shoulder muscles or jaw muscles, or clenching of the teeth. When you identify any of these physical sensations – and the earlier, the better – it is wise to ask yourself 'what am I feeling?' If you cannot immediately identify the feeling, it is best to remove yourself from the threat that is triggering these physical responses until a clearer picture of what you are feeling emerges.

When you become more adept at reading the physical baro-meter to your self-esteem, and begin to listen to the feelings triggering the physical responses, you will gradually be better able to identify particular feelings. Persist until you become expert at identifying your emergency feelings. Once you are able to isolate them when they are at an intense level, you will slowly but surely develop the ability to respond to them at an earlier point.

Many men confuse aggression with anger. Aggression is an action, whereas anger is a feeling. Furthermore, aggression is a loss of self-control and an attempt to control others through fear and threat. Anger is an extremely positive feeling as it not only alerts you to threats to your self-esteem, but also provides the energy for you to take the action needed to cope with the threat.

The earlier you detect emergency feelings when they arise, the easier it is to take constructive action to resolve what is threatening you. Late detection often means being on the edge of loss of control – a precipice from which it can be very difficult to step back.

- Emergency feelings are a message about self

Blaming how you feel on another is a loss of self-control. Examples are: 'you make me angry'; 'you frighten me'; 'you make me sick'. All of these 'you' messages are indirectly and covertly saying something about unmet needs or rights. When you own your own rights, needs and feelings, these 'you' mes-sages would be expressed as 'I' messages: 'I feel angry'; 'I am frightened by your aggressive behaviour'; 'I feel sick when you dismiss how I see things'.

The 'I' message places the reason for communicating on the person sending the message and so is an exercise in self-control. There is a further self-control dimension to an 'I' message, which is that whatever unmet need or right is trig-gering the emergency feeling is the responsibility of the person experiencing it. Parents and teachers have the right to express their feelings and make requests to have certain needs met, but a request must not become a command. There may be many reasons why a student cannot accede to a need of a teacher, and vice versa, but ownership of the unmet need must sit squarely on the shoulders of the person making the request. There is no point in blaming the student who has not been responsive, but there are very strong reasons to pursue other pathways which might secure a positive response.

Understanding the deeper underlying self-aspects of communication is fundamental to the resolution of discipline problems. The more distanced the person is from himself, whether teacher, parent or child, the more likely that passivity, passive-aggression or outright aggression will operate, inevitably leading to discipline problems in homes and schools. Many people live their lives distanced from themselves and this lack of self-possession, self-regard and self-confidence plays havoc with their relationships with others. All communication starts with self and is always fundamentally about self. In your communications with others, the person who most needs to hear your message is yourself. It is a bonus when the other person hears and responds positively to your communication. It is maturity when you yourself hear and act determinedly to fulfil your own needs, wishes and ambitions. The sooner that children are brought to the strong place of self-responsibility and self-relating, the better for them, the people they meet and the places they frequent.

■ Action on emergency feelings

Having identified your emergency feeling and the unmet right or need triggering the feeling and having analysed the deeper self-meaning of the feeling, you are now ready for proaction. Proaction may involve three levels:

- Making a request of another
- Taking ownership of the unmet need or right
- Making a request of self

You have every right to make whatever request you want once you allow the other person to say 'yes' or 'no' to your request. Of course, it makes life considerably easier when reasonable requests are met with mature responses. When this does not happen, then further action is required, but this does not involve annihilating the person who has not positively responded. It does involve ownership of the need and the determination to pursue further ways of having it met. A third level of proaction may be to look at the possibility that your crusade to get others to see and fulfil your needs is masking your own poor action on your needs in life. I have come across crusaders on humanitarian issues who were actually very neglectful of themselves. Their intense and often fundamentalist dedication to the rights and needs of others was a mirror of the deeper need to be dedicated to themselves. Ironically, it is people who are dedicated to their own care that are also most influential in campaigning for the rights of others, because they do so in a way that is calm, reflective, compassionate and respectful of those in opposition to their ideals.

CHAPTER 12

Preventing Discipline Problems

❑ *Prevention in the home*
  - How parents love children
  - How parents parent
  - How parents relate to each other
  - How parents educate children
❑ *Prevention in the school*
  - Reinforcing the positive
  - How teachers relate to students and colleagues
  - How teachers teach

❑ *Prevention in the home*

Parents are not only the primary educators but also the primary disciplinarians of their children. Prevention of discipline problems in the home is a crucial responsibility of parents and involves mainly four areas of interaction:

- How parents love children
- How parents parent
- How parents relate to each other
- How parents educate children

▪ How parents love children

Unconditional love is the deepest longing of all children and is indeed the only mature and healthy type of love.

In unconditional love parents love children for themselves and do not confuse children's behaviours with their wonderful and unique being. One of the most powerful ways to communicate unconditional love is silent holding. Many parents spend too much time doing things with children and little, if any, time being with children. Involving children in multiple academic, sports, musical, artistic and leisure activities does little to convince children of their lovability. Indeed, the children may feel that they are only loved when they are doing something and that just being might be to risk rejection from parents. Children need strong and frequent affirmatory messages that they are loved for themselves and not for what they do. Regrettably, the commonest kind of loving is conditional and many children feel that the means to parental love is being 'good', 'perfect', 'clever', 'obedient', 'quiet', 'beautiful', 'handsome', 'helpless' and so on.

In conditional love children rarely feel loved for their unique persons but they can at least gain recognition for certain behaviours. The extent of conditionality ranges along a continuum from low to extreme. In cases of extreme conditionality parental expectations are very high, and when expectations are not met love can be withdrawn swiftly and harshly. In homes with a low level of conditionality children are primarily seen for themselves but at times love may have to be earned through particular behaviours. The majority of children experience a degree of conditional love that falls between these two poles and this explains why most children have a moderate degree of dependence and insecurity. Such dependence and insecurity are likely to manifest themselves through either under-controlled or over-controlled responses.

There are some homes wherein neither the person nor the behaviour of the children can gain them visibility and love. The parents in these homes have not found love of themselves and their own invisibility to themselves is projected onto their children. Not to be loved is the most despairing experience for children, with consequences of hopelessness, withdrawal, violence, addiction and failed relationships.

■ How parents parent

Nothing is as important to the prevention of discipline problems in the home as the parents' basic concept of parenthood. Commonly assumed roles are the 'benevolent tyrant', the 'controlling protector' and the 'spoiler'. Parents who adopt the role of benevolent tyrant perceive that they have one basic function: to prevent children from doing anything wrong and to punish them when they do. This dominating and critical approach will produce either passivity or rebelliousness on the part of children. Parents who act the role of controlling protector deprive children of opportunities to stand on their own two feet and become self-reliant. These parents show little trust in their children and they emerge from the home fearful, timid, unsure and passive and often become the targets of children who bully. Parents who 'spoil' children give in to their every demand and give them licence to do anything they wish. The children of these parents will lack self-control and can be highly demanding, bossy and unruly.

Parenting is a difficult and complex process and entails knowledge and skills related to the emotional, social, sexual, intellectual, creative, physical and spiritual development of children. It is a role that the majority of parents take on without any preparation or training. This situation is a gross failure on the part of a society that claims it has the welfare of the family at heart. In the absence of training, many parents repeat their own parents' parenting, which may not have been at all desirable. Training in parenting would prevent the onset of many discipline problems in children.

It is the responsibility of anybody who interacts with children to unconditionally love them but it is the sole responsibility of parents to parent them. When parents cannot meet their responsibilities, society needs to have safeguarding structures that uphold the rights of children.

Parenting is largely the task of lovingly equipping children with the knowledge and skills required to cope effectively with each stage of their journey towards adulthood. Effective parenting does not allow children to slide out of the various responsibilities which have to be taken on as they progress towards adulthood. Effective parents not only model appropriate behaviour but offer support and encouragement and are firm in their resolve to get their children to take on their responsibilities. The children of these parents become responsible, self-controlled, mature and self-reliant adults.

Parents need to know how to develop confidence in children and must be aware of the importance of not confusing competence with confidence. They especially need to under-stand the nature of intelligence and to distinguish it from knowledge. Most of all, they must avoid labelling children. The distinction between affirmation and praise is a crucial one, and practice of both processes aids considerably children's self-reliance and self-control. Parents also need to accentuate the positive and firmly and positively correct unwanted behaviours. Parents must not forget to support and reinforce each other's positive parenting efforts.

- ■ How parents relate to each other

Children imitate the behaviours of parents. If, for example, a child witnesses his father frequently berating his mother, he is likely to treat his mother in the same way or he may ally himself with his mother and become her defender by using the tactics of his father. He is then likely to bring these behaviours into the school. A teacher told me a story about a student who was bullying other students and acting aggressively towards teachers. At some stage during an interview with the boy's parents, this teacher noticed the clenched fists and the white knuckles of the father, at which point the father blurted out crossly 'I'll sort out that little fucker'. Wisely, the teacher pointed out to the father that it was now obvious to him where the child's problem was coming from and that really the father needed to resolve his own difficulties before sorting out those of his son.

If a parent is passive and conformist and allows his partner to dominate and control him, there is danger that some of the children will identify with him and take on the same unassertive ways.

Parents need to model appropriate and mature interactions and to apologise when either falls down in that responsibility. Treating each other with respect, making requests rather than commands, owning rather than blaming, being open and spontaneous rather than manipulative and indirect, being warm and supportive rather than dismissive or cold, being provisional rather than dogmatic, and allowing each other the freedom to be different will go a long way towards preventing discipline problems among their children.

Parents need to ensure also that their children interact with each other in respectful and fair ways and must not tolerate any undisciplined conduct between children. This is not a question of taking sides but it is a clear message to children that the family is a place where all members deserve to be loved, valued and communicated with in polite, caring and respectful ways. The message must be that anything short of this will not be tolerated and that the rights of the child who has been the victim of unwanted behaviour will be firmly reinstated.

■ How parents educate children

By the time children come to school they have learned many types of knowledge and to high or low levels. Depending on how parents taught them in the first five years of life, children may have retained their wonderful curiosity and eagerness to learn or they may have become fearful of failure and causing disappointment to parents. When the latter is the case, the children may have creatively invented ways of offsetting criticism and hurt by adopting avoidance strategies, rebelliousness or perfectionism. These protectors against rejection are the bases for many undisciplined behaviours on the part of children:

- Passivity
- Playing truant
- Disruption of class learning
- Attention-seeking
- Shyness and withdrawal
- Reluctance to take on new activities and skills
- Carelessness with class and homework assignments
- Difficulties in forming relationships
- Elective mutism
- Uncooperative behaviour
- Overworking at studies
- Avoidance of school lessons and examinations
- Regular temper tantrums

- Boastfulness
- Destruction of own and others' belongings
- Fearful and timid
- Easily or extremely upset when corrected
- People-pleasing
- Complaining of aches, pains, sickness

Unfortunately, the learning environment in the home often mirrors unhappy learning experiences of the parents themselves in the past and current unhappy school experiences of their children. Parents need to be dedicated to creating a learning environment that is always positive for their children. They need to show interest and commitment in helping their children learn not only academic but also social, emotional, physical and spiritual knowledge and skills. They must particularly avoid the use of ridicule, scolding, corporal punishment, sarcasm, criticism and comparison with others – anything that lessens children's belief in their enormous learning potential or creates alienation from parents. Parents must guarantee that learning will always be done in the presence of love, encouragement, praise, affirmation, belief in children's potential, fun and positive firmness – anything that increases children's belief in themselves and their security of being loved.

Parents, like teachers, need to embrace both failure and success in themselves and in their children and to reward learning efforts; neither failure nor success must be used to motivate children. Parents must also not make the mistake of living their lives through their children's achievements.

Children imitate parents, and when parents show a love of learning, pursue courses of study themselves, set time and space aside for concentrated and focused learning, talk excitedly about what they are doing educationally to the children and calmly approach examinations and assessments, then children will have a tremendous head-start in terms of their educational development.

Parents can also be good models for learning by being reasonably orderly and tidy, by making lists of tasks to be done and ticking off tasks completed and by staying calm.

When parents become frustrated with a task, rather than banging the table or shouting at the children, they can be a model for learning by letting go of the task at that point in time, doing something calming (such as having a cup of coffee, playing a favourite piece of music, going for a walk) and returning later on to the task. When parents become stuck with a task, they can seek help from a knowledgeable source. Children are always observing, and when parents model effective learning strategies, they will pick them up and automatically use them in their own efforts to gain knowledge. All of this modelling reduces the possibility of children reacting to learning, whether in home or school, with undesirable responses.

The following behaviours are important in preventing children developing discipline problems in relation to learning:

- Ensure that learning has only positive associations
- See every effort as an attainment
- Do not confuse effort with performance
- See mistakes and failures merely as stepping-stones for further learning
- View success and failure as relative terms
- Be patient and encouraging of their educational efforts
- Be positively firm in the face of attempts to slide out of learning responsibilities
- Regularly remind them of their limitless intelligence
- Stay relaxed and calm
- Apologise when there is loss of control
- Set up study areas free of distraction
- Help them to do things for themselves
- Help them to be orderly and tidy
- Help them to cope with frustration when learning becomes difficult
- Show them how to make lists of tasks to be done
- Do simple time-management with them
- Teach study skills
- Deal positively with their homework

❑ *Prevention in the school*

It is clear that prevention is far less costly in both human and resource terms than is intervention. Discipline problems among students are certainly lessened by self-discipline among teachers and by teaching and reinforcing self-control in students. Problems are reduced further by having a fair discipline system in place and by frequent reminders of the rights and responsibilities of each member of the school. Apart from these, there are other aspects of teachers' behaviour that can play an important part in the prevention of undesirable behaviours among students:

- How well teachers positively reinforce the disciplined and responsible behaviours of students and colleagues
- How teachers relate to students and colleagues
- How teachers teach

▪ Reinforcing the positive

Children daily show many disciplined behaviours but teachers and parents often fail to reward and reinforce them. Failure to reinforce can lead to a reduction or, indeed, extinction of these desirable behaviours.

Adults need frequently to observe, encourage and reward children's disciplined behaviours in the home and school. In the classroom students demonstrate disciplined behaviour through:

- Attention
- Hard work
- Commitment
- Quietness
- Courtesy
- Endurance
- Cooperation
- Positive responses to requests
- Completed homework
- Order

- Tidiness
- Punctuality
- Speaking in turn

When these disciplined behaviours of children are either verbally or physically reinforced, they are likely to increase in frequency, leading to a lower probability of ill-disciplined behaviours. A mere 'thank you for listening' or 'I appreciate your punctuality' or 'thank you for working so hard' can bring a ray of delight to a student's face and a strengthening of responsible behaviours.

Similarly, teachers need to reinforce each other for disciplined ways of carrying out their responsibilities. Principals, school managers and parents can also be an important source of acknowledgment of the commitment to disciplined behaviour of teachers. Of course, self-praise is the best form of reinforcement of disciplined behaviour. The old saying that 'self-praise is no praise' is misconceived, as the reinforcing feedback of others is only truly heard when firstly you can value your own efforts. Children need to be taught to encourage and reward their own disciplined conduct. When self-reinforcement is present, it becomes a bonus when others praise their genuine efforts at self-control but not something on which they are dependent.

- How teachers relate to students and colleagues

The *sine qua non* of effective teaching is an unconditional loving relationship between the teacher and each student. The prime need of children (and adults) is to be loved. In and outside the school, the loving must always come before the learning. In the past, learning was always deemed more important than liking or loving children. Even more regrettably, love was used as a weapon to either beat children into 'good' behaviour or extinguish 'bad' behaviour. This form of conditional relating plays havoc with children's need for security of love and regard, and most under-controlled and over-controlled responses are by-products of this type of undesirable relating.

Teachers have a responsibility to ensure that the relationship with students is not jeopardised when there are unwanted behaviours on the students' part. This is not a benign issue that teachers can choose to ignore. There is nothing more devastating to a child than the withdrawal of regard because of a piece of unacceptable behaviour. Of course the ill-disciplined reaction must not be ignored, but its correction needs to take place within the context of unconditional regard for the student. The maintenance of regard alongside correction of the difficult response, and reinstatement of the violated right, will lead to a resolution of the problem much more quickly than if the student is put down in a 'tit for tat' exchange.

Not only does the correction of an ill-disciplined behaviour need to be specific to the unwanted response, but also the praise of a desirable behaviour must remain separate from the person to whom the praise is directed. When teachers praise and reward students for their disciplined behaviours, they are confusing person with behaviour and affirmation with praise. When students feel that in teachers' eyes their worth lies in being disciplined and producing high academic results, insecurity is bred and they will either push to please the teacher or rebel against such manipulation. Either way, learning and the relationship with teachers become sources of threat to the students' prime need to be loved.

The confusion of person and behaviour leads to considerable emotional and social insecurity. The person of everyone is unique and immutable and exists before ever behaviour emerges. Behaviour is the means by which you explore the world you live in. Affirmation is the means by which teachers and parents mirror for children their goodness, worth, value, uniqueness, lovability and vast potential. Children become what they are told they are. When, for example, children are labelled as 'weak', 'slow', 'stupid', 'lazy', 'no good', 'a nuisance' or 'incorrigible', they see themselves in that way. Unless their self-image in relation to these areas of behaviour changes, they are unlikely to take control of their troublesome behaviour. Likewise, when children are told regularly and genuinely of their specialness, lovability, wonder, goodness and value, they see themselves in a way that is true to them. This does not mean that you do not correct lack of discipline or shortcomings; to do that would give children an unrealistic self-image. Teachers need to be genuine with students and to communicate to them, in respectful but firm terms, their demand for certain behaviours and their determination to restore any violated rights.

Praise is one of the means used to encourage and reinforce disciplined behaviour, but it is essential that the words of praise are addressed specifically to the desired responses and not to the person of the child. For example, 'I like this essay and I can see that you have put considerable effort into writing it'; there is no judgment here, the behaviour is not enmeshed with the student's person and the hope is that the specific learning effort will increase.

Teachers need too to communicate to students that both their presence and their absence matter. Eye contact, the nod in the student's direction, the wink, the twinkle in the eye, the warm smile, the 'word in the ear' and the genuine greeting all let students know that their presence matters. Equally, the phone enquiry, the welcome back, the look of concern, the words that communicate 'noticed you were missing' and the offer of support and help all communicate that a student's absence matters.

The interrelationships between teachers, principals and school managers need to have the same unconditional quality. Teachers need to feel that their person is always supremely more valued than their behaviour and that both their presence and their absence matter. Furthermore, teachers need affirmation from each other and, particularly, from school leaders. Again, however, it is important that affirmation of a teacher's person is not confused with acknowledgment and praise of teaching and extracurricular efforts. Teachers must not forget that affirmation and praise are two-way processes and that school leaders too need to be recognised and need to have their activities praised.

▪ How teachers teach

There are many adults, including teachers themselves, who have unpleasant memories of their own student days and they still carry feelings of hurt and revenge from that time. Sadly, in the past only a small percentage of adults took up third-level education and one of the primary reasons was gross fear of failure and humiliation in front of others. The fear of failure arises from the fact that it is often followed by criticism, ridicule, scolding, 'put down' messages, comparisons with others, beatings, disappointment and withdrawal of regard. Equally, success can become associated with fear when it is the means of gaining approval, prizes, praise and recognition. Success can mean that high expectations will follow in its train, putting extra pressure on learning and increasing the dreaded possibility of failure.

Both failure and success need to be redeemed from a performance-driven educational system. Many discipline problems have their source in the pressures arising from the fears of failure and success. Some students clearly reduce the possibilities of failure or success by avoidance, apathy, rebelliousness, disruptiveness, conflict and playing truant. Other students get trapped in the performance net and put pressure on themselves to attain ever higher academic standards. These students' emotional and physical well-being is most at risk but, regrettably, they get strongly reinforced in their extreme competitiveness by both teachers and parents.

Most teachers know that failure is a step to learning. However, parents and teachers do not make it safe for children to fail. Both failure and success are integral to the learning process: failure should never have become the stick to beat with or success the carrot to motivate. What counts in learning is effort and this is what needs to be encouraged and praised by teachers. In every effort there is an attainment and it is on that attainment that the next learning effort must rest. It needs to be re-emphasised that the embracing of failure and success as integral and essential aspects of learning and the demonstration of the relative nature of these experiences will go a long way to preventing the onset of discipline problems. The absolute use of the terms failure and success – branding one person a 'failure' and another person a 'success' – is misguided as everyone daily has a mixture of failure and success experiences.

Learning must only have positive associations and sanctions for unwanted behaviour must never involve extra schoolwork or homework. There needs to be an absence of criticism, sarcasm and comparisons with others and the presence of belief in the student and encouragement and praise of all learning efforts. Teachers and parents will do well to remember that all children have limitless potential for learning (human beings only use 2 per cent of their billions of brain cells) and that there is no such phenomenon as grades of intelligence. It is much more accurate to talk about types and levels of knowledge. Depending on the family culture or whether children come from a subculture or from the majority culture, students will come to school with different types and levels of knowledge. They will also have different levels of self-esteem, motivation and inner and outer conflicts. Knowledge must not be confused with intelligence: it must not be assumed that students with a high level of knowledge of, for example, mathematics are more intelligent than those with a lower level of knowledge. Very often the latter children can show higher levels of knowledge in other areas of functioning, for instance sports, physical skills, mechanics, woodwork, social skills, emotional sensitivity, domestic skills, music and art.

Adults must avoid labelling children as 'dull', 'slow', 'weak', 'brilliant', 'average' or 'stupid', because, firstly, these labels are highly inaccurate and have no foundation in reality and, secondly, they totally undermine children's confidence in their potential to learn. Lack of confidence is a source of much under-controlled and over-controlled behaviour. Children mask their lack of confidence with timidity, avoidance or rebellious-ness. Competence blossoms when confidence is firmly rooted in students. Behaviours such as raising students' confidence, encouraging academic efforts and responding positively to failure and success not only make learning a good experience for students but are a major force in preventing discipline problems.

A further issue in the 'how' to teach is to avoid using the red biro: stop emphasising the errors, start marking what has been got right and set the next learning challenge. This positive approach with accurate feedback will enable students to retain the natural curiosity and eagerness to learn that can be observed in babies and toddlers.

Other aspects of teachers' behaviour in the classroom that may prevent difficulties are:

- Having clear rules and expectations that have been agreed on and that are consistently and predictably implemented
- Addressing students by their first names
- Doing careful preparation of classwork
- Being on time for classes and starting immediately
- Including a variety of activities to suit the differences in knowledge levels
- Making requests rather than commands of students
- Finishing class on time and requesting orderly exit
- Closely supervising students
- Observing the effect of their behaviour on students
- Having fair expectations of individual students
- Apologising when a mistake has been made

CHAPTER 13

Resolving Discipline Problems

❑ *When discipline systems fail*
❑ *Resolving discipline problems in the home*
- Unpredictability and inconsistency
- Poor communication
- Double standards
- Lack of sanction room
- Physically or mentally incapacitated parent or child
- Parents with emotional and social difficulties
- Poor marital relationship
- Overprotective parenting
- Dominant parenting
- Emotionless parenting
- Lack of family social outings
- Lack of outside supports

❑ *Resolving discipline problems in the school*
- Poor leadership
- Unpredictability and inconsistency
- Poor communication
- Double standards
- Little or inconsistent involvement of parents
- Undermining of discipline committee
- Poor liaison between monitoring bodies
- Weak staff commitment
- Lack of sanction room
- Burn-out and rust-out of teachers
- Low staff morale
- Students who require specialised help
- Teachers who require specialised help
- Poor preparation and training for new discipline system

❑ *When discipline systems fail*

No matter how persistently rights and responsibilities are declared, individuals are empowered and structures that safeguard rights are created and enacted, it is inevitable that some discipline problems will still emerge.

In examining discipline problems, an important distinction needs to be made between the effects and the causes of ill-disciplined conduct. It is the effects of undisciplined actions that must be the primary target of any discipline system. It has been pointed out that, in general, behaviour is only labelled 'a discipline problem' when it blocks the rights of another. In the immediate situation what needs resolution is not the ill-disciplined behaviour of the perpetrator but the blocked rights of the victim. For example, if a student is the victim of bullying by a teacher, the immediate action that needs to be taken is reinstatement of the student's rights to physical and emotional safety in the classroom. This is the essential element in resolving undisciplined behaviour. Attempts to resolve discipline problems through controlling the perpetrator are unlikely to be successful in reinstating the rights of victims. Accordingly, the focus in this chapter is on the victim.

After reinstatement of the rights of the victim, there is a second issue to be tackled: the psychological rightness on the part of the perpetrator of the ill-disciplined responses. What needs to be discovered is what has led this teacher, student or parent to engage in such socially difficult behaviours and how these behaviours protect the perpetrator. Such an investigation goes beyond discipline (which is about effects on others and is primarily a social phenomenon) to the internal and external causes of ill-disciplined conduct, which is a personal phenomenon. These issues are examined in Part V of the book.

❑ *Resolving discipline problems in the home*

The breakdown of discipline in the home may occur because the discipline system itself is not adequate, but the cause may also lie in other aspects of parenting. It is not the brief of this book to consider the multifaceted nature of parenting,* but

---

* For a detailed exploration of parenting see the author's books, *Self-Esteem: The Key to Your Child's Education* (Dublin: Gill & Macmillan, 1996) and *The Family: Love It and Leave It* (Dublin: Gill & Macmillan, 1996).

what is examined in this chapter are those factors that cause an effective discipline system to break down.

Some of the reasons for the breakdown of a discipline system in the home may also apply in the school; the first four issues listed below fall into this category. There are other more deep-seated reasons for the breakdown of a discipline system in the home; these are concerned primarily with the style of parenting, the physical and emotional well-being of parents and the state of the marital relationship.

- Unpredictability and inconsistency
- Poor communication
- Double standards
- Lack of sanction room
- Physically or mentally incapacitated parent or child
- Parents with emotional and social difficulties
- Poor marital relationship
- Overprotective parenting
- Dominant parenting
- Emotionless parenting
- Lack of family social outings
- Lack of outside supports

▪ Unpredictability and inconsistency

It is vital that, when there are two parents, they are predictable and consistent in following through on the discipline system agreed by the family. Where there are inconsistencies, children learn quickly to play off one parent against another. Sometimes one parent can be 'harder' on one child compared with another; this undermines the system and, even more worrying, leads to the former child feeling less loved than his sibling and the latter being overprotected and allowed to slide out of responsibility.

■ Poor communication

Communication about the discipline code needs to be clear and direct. Many parents complain that telling their children once about what is required should be enough, but the reality is that rights, responsibilities and safeguards need to be repeated frequently – and not only to children.

■ Double standards

Double standards were rampant in the discipline of old. It was deemed okay for adults to shout at and hit children, but children dared not counter those abusive actions with similar responses. Similarly, it was considered fitting that children be sanctioned for breaking rules, but no such safeguarding sanctions existed for parents. Discipline is for all members of the family and when parents accept this they are more likely to be effective in implementing a fair discipline system.

■ Lack of sanction room

Just as a designated sanction room in the school is necessary to safeguard teachers and students, so too its existence in the home is essential to safeguarding the rights of parents and children in the face of undisciplined behaviour.

■ Physically or mentally incapacitated parent or child

In families where there is a physically or mentally incapacitated parent, the children may run riot or become adults too soon or the responsibility of parenting may lay too heavily on the shoulders of the healthy parent. This is a difficult family situation and fair allocation of roles and the employment of outside supports are necessary to keep this family on a healthy path. Similar outcomes can ensue where there is a child in the family who is physically or mentally disadvantaged. It is often the case that the other children in such a family are too strictly parented and given unfair responsibilities at too early an age. Parents are often too lenient on the child who is incapacitated, who then fails to learn control over his actions, and double standards are created for the other children.

■ Parents with emotional and social difficulties

Parents bring their emotional baggage into the family and they can, for example, be depressed, highly anxious, obsessive-compulsive, perfectionistic or addicted to drugs, alcohol, food, work or relationships. Parents with such emotional problems are in no position to parent effectively or to create an effective discipline system. These parents need professional help and, in the meantime, schools, churches, voluntary bodies, communities and health authorities must do their utmost to care for and safeguard the rights of the children and the other parent in this family.

■ Poor marital relationship

It is the sad story of our times that a high percentage of marriages break down. It is also the case that a high percentage of intact relationships are troubled. When there is division between parents, it inevitably results in a divided family: some children form an alliance with the father and others with the mother. In such a case the discipline system can become a weapon for the unhappy couple to wield at each other, and the security of the family suffers further threat. Whether the couple resolve their difficulties or choose to part, marital turmoil does not have to mean family discord. Parents, whether living together or apart, have a responsibility to maintain family harmony and effective discipline. It is an established fact that women who are left with the care of adolescent sons have many discipline problems because they do not receive support and input from the fathers. Children need their one-to-one relationship with each parent and they also need the security of experiencing the same discipline expectations from each of the parents. It is important too that parents are disciplined in their responses to each other and to the children.

■ Overprotective parenting

Overprotective parenting arises when parents are dependent on their children and want them to love them, whatever the cost. It can also arise from one parent protecting the children from an aggressive and critical parent. Overprotected children are allowed slip out of responsibilities, and because they develop neither the self-confidence nor the competence to cope with all the demands of the world, they become dependent on and highly demanding of others. These children can present as troublesome, aggressive and uncooperative in the school. No effective discipline operates in the home that is overprotective.

▪ Dominant parenting

Where there is dominant parenting, too little is expected of the parents and too much of the children. These are parents who live their lives through their children's looks, abilities and achievements. 'Shoulds', 'should nots', 'have tos' and 'ought tos' dominate interactions in this family. The atmosphere is strained, tense and fearful. The discipline system is likely to be authoritarian and applied only to the children. The children may grow up competent in certain areas of functioning but they will lack self-confidence and have serious doubts about their lovability.

Dominating parents have a responsibility to resolve their own dependencies and to learn more caring ways of parenting and disciplining. They also need to accept that discipline is not a practice just for children.

In the school, children of dominating parents tend to be conformist, submissive, passive, shy, perfectionist, eager to please and fearful of failure. Sometimes a child will rebel against this type of parenting, but he has then learned to fight fire with fire and becomes undisciplined like his parents. This child can be quite difficult to handle in school, but the responsibility needs to be placed firmly on the parents.

▪ Emotionless parenting

This is a sad family to contemplate where children, in spite of their best efforts, cannot gain love and recognition. There is no more devastating plight for a child or adult than to live in a world without love, and where this is so discipline is the furthest thing from the person's mind and heart. The children of loveless homes can be violent, aggressive, irresponsible, depressed, hopeless, attention-seeking or addicted to drugs or alcohol; they can also manifest their despair through isolation, obsessive-compulsive behaviours, apathy and attempted suicide. They are rarely responsible and disciplined.

Both parents and children in this situation need considerable professional help. The children are unlikely to adapt to the order and routine of school until the disorder of the world of their families is corrected. Whilst schools need to show care for these children, they cannot totally heal their wounded hearts and, moreover, they cannot allow these children to block the development of others.

■ Lack of family social outings

It may seem unusual to note lack of social outings as a cause of the failure of discipline systems in the home but it is a situation that indicates poor family morale. When there is little interaction between the members of the family and no social outings, the motivation to be disciplined in their responses towards each other is easily eroded. Families that plan, create, problem-solve, pray and play together are far more likely to be loyal to an agreed discipline system.

It is more than likely in this situation that parenting skills are weak and that parents rarely talk or interact with others.

■ Lack of outside supports

Healthy families have strong contacts outside the family, such as friendships, extended family, support groups, community and church associations and sports clubs. Some families will not allow anybody inside the door and will not countenance outside contacts. This puts intolerable strain on the family to meet all the needs of its members, and when the inevitable crises develop these families do not cope very well. The children of these families tend to be insular, lack social skills and stand out as unusual among their peers. They normally will not cause discipline problems themselves but they can become victims of teachers or students who bully.

❑ *Resolving discipline problems in the school*

Discipline problems in schools only exist when there are weaknesses in the structures that safeguard the rights of all those in the system. There will always be individual teachers, parents and students who come into the school with moderate to very high degrees of vulnerability, but the discipline system should ensure that their problems do not disrupt the lives of others. A system that goes beyond discipline (see Chapter 14) is needed to resolve the personal, family and interpersonal difficulties of such individuals, but caring for the perpetrators of ill-disciplined conduct must not be enmeshed with the vindication of the rights of others in the school.

When, in spite of the presence of a sophisticated and caring discipline system, the rights of teachers or students continue to be threatened, then a thorough investigation of the violations should unearth the weaknesses in the discipline system. It is not individual students or teachers who are at fault; rather the system is somehow failing to safeguard its members in certain circumstances. Clearly, when the discipline system is weak and ill-thought-out, the resolution of continuing discipline problems lies in the development of and the commitment to a well-structured, impartial and fair discipline system.

The main reasons why well-structured discipline systems may not prove totally effective are:

- Poor leadership
- Unpredictability and inconsistency in applying the discipline system
- Poor communication of the discipline system
- Existence of double standards
- Little or inconsistent involvement of parents
- Discipline committee undermined by principal or staff members
- Poor liaison between discipline committee and student committee and between these two committees and parents' association and board of management
- Weak staff commitment to implementation of the discipline system

- Lack of sanction room
- Burn-out and rust-out of teachers
- Low staff morale
- Presence of students who require either a different type of school or specialised education
- Teachers who require professional help
- Poor preparation and training for new discipline system

Each school must try to detect the failures in its particular discipline system. Identification of the failures or weaknesses is the foundation for creating a stronger system of care and discipline.

■ Poor leadership

The principal and vice-principal are the main architects of the culture of the school. An effective discipline system should be able to identify and allow for proaction where there is poor leadership. Teachers have tended to shy away from confrontation on ineffective leadership for fear of retaliation, victimisation and ostracisation. But these responses are further violations of teachers' rights, and the discipline system must ensure there are structures to safeguard teachers against such actions. When the breakdown of a discipline system is due to poor leadership and teachers' passivity in the face of it, then correction of these two issues is needed urgently. There is no point in teachers blaming the principal, who is doing her best within the limits of her vulnerability. Teachers must put their energy into the aspects of the discipline system that confront poor leadership and empower them to assert their rights. When the leader refuses to cooperate, then actions that go over her head are needed until the rights of teachers, students and parents are once again held sacred.

■ Unpredictability and inconsistency

A school can devise an excellent system of discipline but unpredictable and inconsistent implementation can sabotage its effectiveness. Predictability in a discipline system means that no matter how small or large is the infringement of a person's right, immediate action will always take place to reinstate the violated right. Unpredictability blurs boundaries, and perpetrators of undisciplined actions will push until they hit the strong and solid boundary wall of the other person's right. Consistency means that the system is applied equally across all individuals, situations and times of year. Inconsistency arises where certain students or teachers are more targeted than others, or particular teachers or students apply the system only in particular situations or for 'more serious' infringements of rights. Indifference to apparently 'less serious' infringements is a serious weakness in a discipline system and only serves to perpetuate and possibly escalate unacceptable conduct.

It is important that both the discipline committee and the student committee closely monitor whether the system is being applied predictably and consistently and that they act quickly and firmly if there is any falling short on these two essential aspects of safeguarding the rights of all. When an individual teacher is failing in either aspect, confrontation is necessary. The confrontation needs to take the form of querying the undesirable practices, insisting on the responsibility to apply discipline procedures and helping the teacher to re-establish predictability and consistency. This may involve some opportunities for personal empowerment work and the support of colleagues for the teacher to firmly implement the agreed discipline system.

Similarly, when an individual student is not reporting unacceptable behaviours on the part of teachers or fellow students, he needs empowering and support to vindicate his own rights and those of others.

■ Poor communication

A well-designed discipline system may come apart at the seams because of either initial poor communication to those concerned or lack of follow-up communication to reinforce its implementation. Sometimes new or substitute teachers or students starting the academic year later than peers may not be fully appraised of the discipline system and their responses to difficult situations may not be in keeping with the school's discipline approach. Regular meetings of staff and student committees on discipline issues should guard against such communication difficulties.

■ Double standards

Teachers are notorious for operating double standards when applying discipline procedures. It is okay for them to swiftly and firmly safeguard their rights in the face of students' difficult behaviours, but it is not equally okay for students to act in a similar way when they are faced with undesirable responses from teachers. Such unfairness will weaken students' commitment to respecting the rights of teachers. Students respond well when there is equal treatment for all members of the school. Double standards may ensue if students have not been sufficiently empowered and given strong, direct and clear permission to voice dissatisfactions with their teachers. But whatever the reasons for double standards emerging, the state of 'one law for all' must be restored for the discipline system to survive and thrive.

■ Little or inconsistent involvement of parents

Parental involvement is the cornerstone of an effective school discipline system. Their belief in, support for and reinforcement of the system will make it more likely that students will adapt to the school policies. It has already been mentioned that the persistent discipline offender, more often than not, comes from a troubled home. The education and involvement of these parents is crucial, not only for their children's overall development, but for the responsible caring by their children of others in the school. Teachers need to let go of their resistance to parental involvement in school matters and instead harness parents' expertise, commitment and support for their own and their students' welfare.

When students witness a split between parents and teachers on discipline demands they can quickly exploit it and resist the safeguarding structures. It is important that they are not allowed to do this, but it is even more important to secure the cooperation of parents. When parents fail to cooperate, responsibility for their children's violations of the rights of others must be laid squarely back on their shoulders. This may ultimately involve suspension or expulsion of the student for the sake of everyone, including the student and the parents.

■ Undermining of discipline committee

The discipline committee can sometimes be undermined because a principal or vice-principal makes unilateral decisions that are contrary to the recommendations of the committee. Such breaking of ranks must be confronted. The principal may argue that she had information to which the discipline committee was not privy, but this does not justify non-consultative actions. The discipline committee requires the steadfast support of the principal, vice-principal, other teachers, the parents' association and the board of management. If people have misgivings or reservations on its decisions and policies, then there must be dialogue with the committee. No system or aspect of it can be changed without involving all the designers of the system.

■ Poor liaison between monitoring bodies

There are a number of monitoring bodies in the school system: board of management, parents' association, discipline committee and student committee. Each of these needs to know what the others are doing. There may be a temptation on the part of teachers to liaise less frequently with the student committee and, possibly, the parents' association, but lack of liaison may well be the sword that the discipline system falls on. Student involvement and support are vital to the effectiveness of a discipline system, as is the back-up of parents. The more frequent and meaningful the contacts between the various monitoring bodies, the stronger the discipline system.

■ Weak staff commitment

There are school staffs where unresolved hurts and grievances, very often of many years' standing, dog the creation of an effective discipline system. Troubled staffs are often reflected in cliques, uncooperative behaviour, resentment and fears of judgment and ridicule. Some schools are now availing of professional facilitators to help bring these issues out into the open and resolve them. No discipline system will survive serious difficulties among staff members. For their own welfare and that of students and parents, and for the image of the school, leaders and teachers must take on the responsibility of healing 'dis-eased' staff relationships. The rewards are great: a more cohesive and caring staff and a more effective discipline system.

Weak staff commitment can arise because government and the school inspectorate fail to recognise the needs of teachers and place too great an emphasis on academic performance as a measurement of school effectiveness. An attitude of 'why should we care when they don't show care?' can be easily engendered by bureaucratic management.

Poor commitment can also arise where there is an ageing staff who have been indoctrinated into the authoritarian style of classroom management and either are too insecure or feel it is too late to change to an effective discipline system. Government and the school inspectorate seriously need to consider ways of updating these teachers' ways of communicating or help them to move on to an alternative career within the public service. Their presence on a school staff can cripple new developments.

■ Lack of sanction room

Most schools seem to find it extremely difficult to provide a sanction room. This can be due to sheer lack of space, but more often it is because the priority of having a sanction room is not appreciated.

■ Burn-out and rust-out of teachers

Burn-out is a common condition among teaching staffs. Typical symptoms are fatigue, absenteeism, loss of appetite, insomnia, hatred of teaching, depression, pessimism, psychosomatic complaints (for example, headaches, back and shoulder pain, stomach aches), low self-esteem, low motivation and low creativity. Teachers who are burned out will not have the energy or motivation to cooperate with new school policies, and unless the underlying reasons for their burn-out are dealt with, their presence on a staff will militate against progressive changes.

One of the underlying sources of burn-out is the teacher's enmeshment of her identity with her profession and consequent compensation strategies to maintain her image through teaching. This is an insecurity that bedevils many people and one that is often regarded as virtuous. However, whereas the school and students may initially benefit from such a teacher's overdedication and commitment, the teacher herself, her family and marriage may suffer greatly. Because the role demands in teaching continue to increase, teachers who are perfectionistic can burn out quite quickly in their efforts to stem the tide of failure-to-cope.

There is a failure of leadership when teachers burn out rather than have their symptoms recognised earlier on and have appropriate help offered. Very often principals value those teachers highly and are wont to load them with extra responsibilities as they are highly efficient and are unlikely to say 'no'.

'Rust-out' is the opposite of burn-out but it is equally common and its consequences are equally serious. Whereas the people who suffer burn-out have exhausted themselves in the 'pursuit of excellence', teachers with rust-out lose motivation very early on in their career when the profession does not measure up to expectations. If compensation and perfectionism mark the teacher who burns out, avoidance and apathy are the characteristics of the teacher who rusts out.

These teachers pose a difficult challenge for school management as they tend to miss staff meetings, hate teaching, deride proposals for change, create a clique of like-minded colleagues and avoid staff development days and social outings. They need considerable personal help to regain motivation, and the system has to be firm in not inflicting them on other staff and on students. To ignore their condition is an act of neglect of them, their colleagues, students and their parents. Government must find some mechanism to help these at-risk teachers; for example, offer them a post in another branch of the public service or provide confidential counselling.

- Low staff morale

Low staff morale is characterised by unilateral decision-making, poor level of staff interaction, cliques, hostility, fear, non-cooperation, poor availability and low approachability of leaders, and little or no affirmation or praise. This is a very 'dis-eased' situation, and here the resolution of discipline problems, whilst important, must take second place to the resolution of staff relationships. Professional facilitation, individual counselling and staff training in such topics as stress, communication, self-esteem and relationships may be required to move the staff to a welfare place. Boards of management, parents' associations, the school inspectorate and government must do everything in their power to resolve such an intolerable situation.

- Students who require specialised help

Some schools are given responsibility for students who are deeply insecure and distressed, who come from troubled homes or who may be members of a subculture. When, in spite of the school's best efforts, these children do not adapt to the culture of the school, and pose a serious threat to order in the school, then alternative means of education may be required. Certainly, the problems of the students must not jeopardise the rights of others in the school. It is misguided to keep these children in the school if no benefits are accruing from their participation. This is an issue that principals, in particular, may need to be brave on, since lack of action means everybody gets neglected. It may be that professional help can be provided, and only when the children are ready to adapt to the school culture should they be returned to it. It is recommended that the school maintains contact with children who are not attending school.

- Teachers who require specialised help

There may also be teachers in the school who have deep personal and interpersonal difficulties that require professional intervention. When their coping problems block the rights of students and colleagues, it becomes expedient that they are confronted on the necessity of resolving their unhappy state. Just as for students, the personal difficulties of teachers cannot be allowed to threaten the welfare of others. Regrettably, such teachers have been allowed to either terrorise and intimidate children or be apathetic in their teaching duties. School management needs to be empowered by the Department of Education to confront these teachers sensitively but firmly and only allow them to return to active teaching when they are in a position to respect and uphold their own rights and those of students and colleagues.

- Poor preparation and training for new discipline system

It may be difficult for teachers who have operated in either an authoritarian or a passive style to suddenly take on the assertive style of the system of discipline being proposed in this book. Training on all the levels of the system is essential, especially determining responses to hypothetical scenarios (for example, if a student spits at a teacher). Access to a safe forum when difficulties arise in implementing the system and, most of all, the back-up support of management and colleagues are needed. Patience and persistence also help.

PART V

Beyond Discipline

CHAPTER 14

Responding to the Cries for Help

❑ *Beyond discipline*
❑ *Responding to the cries for help of children*

- How teachers relate to the student
- How other students relate to the student
- Student's need for approval
- How parents relate to the student
- Low self-esteem
- Unsuitable school

❑ *Responding to the cries for help of parents*
❑ *Responding to the cries for help of teachers*

- Evaluation of and change in staff relationships
- Evaluation of and change in the behaviours of leaders
- Updating of teaching and classroom management skills
- Personal counselling
- An honourable way out of teaching

❑ *Beyond discipline*

Parents, teachers and children do not engage in unwanted behaviours to make life difficult for others. They do so because their fundamental rights have not and are not being met and because responsible behaviours on their part previously have not gained them respect. As a result, they are forced into adopting actions that are 'cries for help' either to gain positive responses to their needs or to reduce further experiences of hurt and rejection.

Adults and children who are under-controlled or over-controlled in their everyday behaviour are deeply unhappy and tormented. Whilst their difficult behaviours cannot be allowed to block the rights of others, it must be seen that they are as much victims of neglect as those they offend. Discipline is about safeguarding the rights of victims, but homes and schools must go beyond discipline and attempt to heal the deprivations and hurts of those who perpetrate undesirable actions.

When it comes to children who are troublesome, parents and people in authority in particular need to explore the causes of the cry for help of the unwanted actions. Children themselves need to be given a safe forum to express their hurts, grievances and low self-esteem. Teachers and parents need also to evaluate whether these children may themselves be victims of other children who tease, taunt and bully them. When teachers' undisciplined conduct is being considered, colleagues, principals and school managers need to seriously look at staff relationships. However, the teachers themselves may be carrying their own emotional baggage into the school and loading it onto the shoulders of students and colleagues. Similarly, parents who violate the rights of children and others must look at their home of origin and see whether they are repeating or compensating for the hurts experienced there. They may need to evaluate their parenting skills and their relationship with their partners.

Compassion and understanding are the basic responses needed to heal the hurts of those who either lash out or withdraw from a world that has left them bruised and feeling unwanted. Judgment, condemnation, superiority and blaming violate their rights and only serve to deepen their hurts. Furthermore, judgmental reactions are themselves ill-disciplined and only fight fire with fire.

It is necessary to go beyond discipline if the causes of discipline problems are to be resolved. The focus in this process is on the child, parent or teacher who perpetrates violations of the rights of others. The aim is to discover the rights that have been violated in their own lives and find ways of resolving those losses. Whilst this chapter focuses largely on the school context, the issues raised and the principles underlying the 'beyond discipline' response apply equally to the home context.

❑ *Responding to the cries for help of children*

The first 'beyond discipline' response needed from teachers in relation to students who are undisciplined is to ask themselves: 'what are the underlying reasons for this particular student's difficult behaviours?' Teachers need to recognise that the undisciplined behaviour of any one student has a unique protective and alerting function for that student. Furthermore, teachers must be wary of assuming that what helped one student will help another.

There are several possible sources of undisciplined behaviour among students:

- How teachers relate to the student
- How other students relate to the student
- Student's need for approval
- How parents relate to the student
- Low self-esteem
- Unsuitable school

■ How teachers relate to the student

Many teachers may pinpoint a troubled home as the source of the cry for help. However, while this may be so, it must not deflect teachers from also examining the way they themselves interact with the undisciplined student. Teachers would be wise to ask themselves the following questions so that they might begin the healing process:

- Do I treat this student with respect?
- Do I address this student by his preferred title?
- Do I make fair requests?
- Are my academic expectations realistic?
- Do I 'put down' this student?

- Do I communicate directly and clearly?
- Do I request rather than order?
- Do I correct misbehaviour in a way that does not jeopardise my relationship with the student?
- Am I prepared to give help when the student is academically struggling?
- Do I compare this student with others?
- Do I ever employ cynicism and sarcasm?
- Do I listen?
- Do I regularly affirm the unique person of this student?
- Do I encourage and praise academic and social efforts?
- Do I notice when this student is absent?
- Do I view mistakes and failures as opportunities for learning?
- Do I value success above academic efforts?

The answers to these questions can alert teachers to whether their ways of relating to the student may be precipitating protective responses. Whether the primary sources of the problem are in the home or in the classroom, a positive relationship with teachers will always benefit the student's security and self-esteem.

■ How other students relate to the student

Student and discipline committees need to be alert to the fact that students can suffer greatly at the hands of fellow students. Children who are bullied or ostracised by peers may take their frustration out on younger children or teachers. They may also become withdrawn and depressed and their attention to schoolwork may be seriously weakened. Some types of bullying can be very subtle (for example, notes, hints, avoidance), but their effects can be devastating. The school and home must ensure loudly and clearly that there is permission to speak out about such damaging behaviour and that such revelations are seen as acts of strength. Furthermore, reports of bullying, when verified, must be acted on quickly and decisively. An increase in the intensity of supervision of interactions between the victim and perpetrators must follow identification of the culprits. Some healing questions to be asked are:

- How does this troubled student get on with his peers?
- How do his peers interact with him?
- Does he have any friends?
- Does he participate in informal and formal games?
- What is his manner of talking – aggressive, boastful, timid, shy, fearful, passive?
- In group dynamics who, if anyone, chooses him as a partner?
- With whom does he arrive to school?
- With whom does he leave school?
- Is there evidence of bullying?

▪ Student's need for approval

Children go through stages in verifying their worth in the eyes of other people. The first test is how their parents relate to them, then adult relatives and neighbours, later on brothers and sisters, and in middle childhood other children. In adolescence they have a need to be accepted by their own gender group, later the need for a bosom pal and later again the need for acceptance by the opposite sex peer group. The final conquest is a full relationship with a peer. All through adolescence the need for acceptance from teachers is also important. When students, for whatever reasons, miss out on these important milestones of security and self-esteem, they can present undisciplined behaviour such as moodiness, hostility, self-absorption, obsessiveness or withdrawal.

There are students who put major pressure on themselves to attain high academic performance as a means of gaining their parents' approval. These students can sometimes be hostile, be easily upset and 'act out' under academic pressure.

There are other students who will do anything to win the approval of peers; they may act as daredevils, try to 'put one over' on the teacher, act the bully or be the 'funny person' who raises a laugh in the classroom. These students tend to form cliques or gangs and can make painful the lives of students outside their group. Teachers find these students difficult to handle, as the attention of peers counts more strongly than that of the teacher. Moreover, many other students reinforce these students' behaviours out of fear of becoming their victims in order to hide their own fears and vulnerabilities.

The student committee has a vital role to play in helping these troubled students. The committee must make it plainly known that these students are accepted for themselves and that they do not have to go to the undesirable lengths they do in order to gain acceptance. The committee must find ways of sanctioning the undesirable behaviours whilst maintaining connection with the students, and they must also ensure that other students do not reinforce any behaviours of these students that transgress the rights of others.

The discipline committee needs to support the student committee in helping these students to feel recognised and wanted for themselves and not for what they do. Teachers need to ensure that they do not get trapped into conflict with these students in the process of safeguarding their own and other students' rights.

■ How parents relate to the student

In many instances of undisciplined behaviour the cause lies deeply in the student's home circumstances. The questions that the concerned teacher, principal or discipline committee needs answers to are:

- What is the nature of the mother's relationship to the student?
- What is the nature of the father's relationship to the student?
- Do both parents agree on discipline procedures?
- Is there a sick or troubled parent in this home?
- Is this a two- or a three-generation family?
- Is the student presenting problems at home?
- What do the parents consider are the reasons for the difficult behaviour at school?
- Is there sibling rivalry?
- Is there any violence towards the student?
- Is there any possibility of intimidation by adults other than parents?
- Do parents feel they can trust the childminder?

- Is there any display of unusual behaviours at home (for example, sexual preoccupation, frequent checking of plugs, switches and locks, excessive hand-washing, bullying of younger siblings)?
- Do the parents have unrealistic academic expectations of the troubled student?

Parents will not answer these questions honestly unless they feel safe in the company of whoever is interviewing them. The approach must be non-judgmental, compassionate and understanding, and there must be acknowledgement of the need for their help and cooperation. Care for them and the student will go a long way towards helping these parents to open up on their own shortcomings and their need for help. If the student is being removed from the classroom, it must be emphasised to the parents that he cannot be allowed to return to class until some resolution has been achieved, and the parents need to be helped to see that this is an act of caring. It can be pointed out that the student was not gaining from being in class and will not do so until the emotional difficulties are healed. The immediate priority is not this student's education but his emotional, social and, perhaps, physical well-being. Educational progress follows on these more fundamental securities.

There are a number of options that schools can make available for this family:

- Personal and confidential counselling for the student
- Family counselling
- Couple counselling
- Parenting counselling or courses
- Frequent liaison with student counsellor (with student's permission)
- Frequent liaison with home–school liaison officer
- Joint management strategy between school and home with direct involvement of the student
- Tutorials for areas of knowledge in which student has fallen behind

Persistence and patience on all sides are required to help gain the trust of such troubled students. Because the student is out of class does not mean that teachers no longer have a responsibility to show love and care – indeed the contrary is very much the case. It is now more than any other time that the student needs teachers and peers to stand by him.

■ Low self-esteem

How a child views self has a great influence on how he will behave in home and school. When children see themselves as 'bad' or 'slow' or 'weak' or 'stupid' or 'ugly', they will act in accordance with these labels through either under-controlled or over-controlled behaviours. Unless attention is paid to their feelings about themselves, it is unlikely any improvement in their difficult behaviours will occur.

■ Unsuitable school

For their own image purposes, some parents have children attending schools that do not suit the children's interests. These children can experience considerable academic failure, and become disillusioned and thorns in the sides of teachers and other students. Often, finding a school that matches their interests can lead to a revitalisation of motivation to learn and an elimination of discipline problems.

❏ *Responding to the cries for help of parents*

Health and social agencies have tended to be judgmental and harsh in their response to parents' undisciplined actions towards children. Parents never wittingly hurt their children: but from their own unhealed abuse and hurt experiences, they in turn can unwittingly hurt children. When they have not received love, how can they give it? When they have been victims of physical, sexual or emotional abuse, how can they provide tenderness and gentleness? When their worth was measured by conformity to certain behavioural expectations, how can they be unconditional in their loving of children? Parents need healing of their own wounds before they can heal the wounds they have inflicted on their children. Schools can play a crucial role in helping these parents find the help they so dearly need. Teachers' compassionate and caring responses to these parents may be the first acts of caring they receive and may well launch them on the road to recovery.

The school, the community and the church must not only attempt to share the rearing of the at-risk children of these distressed parents but also provide love, care and tangible help for the parents themselves:

- Personal psychotherapy (a list of recognised practitioners could be got from the school's doctor)
- Couple counselling
- Family therapy
- Parenting courses
- Personal support from home–school liaison officer or guidance counsellor
- Support groups (parents' association, Parentline)
- Respite from parenting service
- Adult evening classes
- Courses on adult stress, self-esteem, communication, assertiveness, relationships
- Provision of reading materials on parenting, couple relationships, children's education, self-esteem, personal development

❏ *Responding to the cries for help of teachers*

Teachers who exhibit undisciplined behaviours of either an aggressive or passive nature are crying out for help for underlying problems such as low self-esteem, unresolved conflicts from childhood, dependence on others and fears of failure. These teachers may need help in one or more of a number of directions:

- Evaluation of and change in staff relationships
- Evaluation of and change in the behaviours of the school leaders
- Updating of teaching and classroom management skills
- Personal counselling
- Provision of an honourable way out of teaching

■ Evaluation of and change in staff relationships

The source of aggression or passivity among teachers may very well lie in a non-supportive and critical working environment. Many teachers are left isolated in their classrooms, dare not ask for help and are bereft of effective leadership. Changes in staff morale, staff relationships and leadership are vital to healing the problematic behaviours of the troubled teacher. In some schools, professional facilitators are now brought in to heal long-standing problems among staff. A lot more needs to be done in the creation of structures that teachers can have recourse to in the face of a principal or staff members who are reluctant to entertain change. An accountability system needs to exist to handle principals who may be rigid, inflexible or passive. Teachers need to be able to seek help from somebody or some system outside the school that will act on their behalf.

■ Evaluation of and change in the behaviours of leaders

When the source of an individual teacher's coping problems lies in ineffective leadership, then it is incumbent on the school leaders to honestly evaluate how they relate to this particular staff member. I have worked with individual teachers who had been intimidated and threatened whenever they attempted to raise their own rights or the rights of others. Many felt their jobs were at risk. These teachers felt profoundly unsafe about voicing any concerns and silently bore the brunt of unfair decisions and responsibilities. Principals and managers are the architects of the school culture, and actions which perpetuate a reign of fear and intimidation or apathy and passivity can no longer be tolerated. Not only is the particular teacher who is a victim of these responses in need of help, but the leaders themselves must also seek help. It is well to remember that people who show no caring of others rarely show care of themselves either.

Principals who are not successful in achieving good staff morale may point to high academic results or highly modernised equipment and buildings as evidence of effectiveness. Leadership certainly involves helping children maximise their educational opportunities in well-equipped schools, but the real test of leadership is the relationships that principals create with teachers, students and parents. Many principals need training in a management style that is caring and transformational in nature. Transformational leadership is based on the premise that responsible leaders can empower those in the school and foster a work life that is meaningful and satisfying to all members of the school.

Transformational leadership creates a work environment based on the following beliefs:

- Teachers and students have immense potential and given the right circumstances will work hard to apply it.
- Teachers and students are honest and trustworthy; they want and deserve to be treated with respect and dignity.
- Teachers and students understand the purpose of their work and the goals of the school.
- All members of the school and the parents of the students are accountable.
- Teachers, students, parents and management are able to identify and learn from mistakes and problems before they escalate or are transferred to higher levels of the educational system.
- Principals and managers are responsible for acquainting teachers, students and parents with the working of the school.
- Leaders are responsible for ensuring that information is shared and communicated in a two-way process.
- Leaders, teachers, students and parents have a responsibility to each other. This responsibility translates into a sense of values, empathy, understanding, caring and mutual support.

Transformational leadership creates a school where teachers and students believe in and care about their work. It provides challenges by emphasising solutions to problems, and it encourages individual growth, self-knowledge and physical, social and spiritual enhancement. Principals and managers who follow this philosophy lead with both the head and the heart.

Transformational leaders possess:

- A clear vision of how they want the school to be
- The capacity to communicate this vision and gain the support of teachers, students and parents
- Persistency, consistency and focus, particularly when undisciplined conduct arises
- The capacity to empower staff, students and parents to work towards their individual and collective goals; the emphasis is on self-responsibility, questioning and changing limiting beliefs and the development of a sense of spiritual self
- The capacity to employ innovative ideas and practices that enable the school to monitor its progress, past and present, and its overall effectiveness

Transformational leaders are perpetual learners who learn from their own and others' experiences. Effective leaders know that learning is the mainspring of effectiveness, the source of energy that maintains dynamism by continually triggering new understanding, new ideas and new challenges.

Teachers who are victims of ineffective leaders would do well to seek out ways of empowering themselves and to ally themselves with other teachers who are unwilling to conform to the untenable situation. Eventually, teachers will need to say 'no' to the unacceptable actions of ineffective leaders. In any case, justice will prevail as the problems lie with the leaders and not with their victims.

■ Updating of teaching and classroom management skills

Individual teachers may resort to undisciplined conduct because they are relying on teaching and classroom techniques that students will no longer tolerate. These teachers need skills training that matches the changing wider culture of their students. It is incumbent on the state to ensure that training courses match both the individual and group needs of teachers and the unique culture of the school.

■ Personal counselling

Reflection is central to maturity. People who go through life without ever evaluating how they are with themselves, with others and with work can doom themselves to a dark existence of dependence and vulnerability. Many teachers are now seeking the help of psychotherapists, clinical psychologists and counsellors. Teachers who engage in either over-controlled or under-controlled reactions to students and colleagues have a responsibility to seek professional help to resolve their long-standing inner difficulties. They can no longer impose their problems on students and colleagues, and a break from teaching may be necessary for them until they have largely resolved their emotional difficulties. The Department of Education needs to create a confidential and free counselling service for teachers.

The criteria for selection of entrants to the teaching profession is an area that teacher training colleges may need to examine more closely. High academic results or teaching skills do not necessarily lead to effective teaching. How the person relates personally and interpersonally should be crucial criteria for admission to the profession.

■ An honourable way out of teaching

There are some teachers who have lost all motivation for the job, and these should be provided with an exit out of teaching without loss of face. Teachers have many skills that could transfer to other areas of the public service, and a short training could equip them for a position befitting their age and experience. It is important that they do not experience the move as a demotion and they must not suffer any loss of earnings. Such flexibility would benefit other areas of the public service. Furthermore, the loss to society is far greater when teachers retire on sickness grounds or show high levels of absenteeism over several years.

CHAPTER 15

Caring Homes and Schools

- ❑ *Creating communities of care*
- ❑ *Caring homes*
  - Caring for parents
  - Caring for children
- ❑ *Caring schools*
  - Caring for teachers
  - Caring for students
  - Caring for parents

❑ *Creating communities of care*

The ultimate aim of every social or educational system must
be to care for every aspect of the development of each of its
members. Nobody would dispute that families are there for
the welfare of all their members. Some might dispute that
schools are, or need to be seen as, communities of care.
Certainly, many teachers feel that schools have not been
solicitous about their needs and many students feel that
examination results count more than their unique, sacred and
endlessly creative selves. In families, many parents feel they do
not matter in the eyes of their partners or children and many
children feel loved not for themselves but only for conformity
to their parents' expectations of them. Childminders, too,
often feel undervalued by parents and, sometimes, the children
for whom they care.

The more that principals, teachers, students, government
and teachers' unions view the school as a place of care for all
its members, the greater will be the progress on the discipline
and 'beyond discipline' systems proposed in this book. The
narrow view of the school as purely an educational setting has
not worked and will never work. When teachers and students
come to school they leave behind neither their rights and
needs nor the emotional baggage of their self-esteem difficulties

200

and dependence on others. Compassion, understanding, safety and opportunities for growth and change are vital if a school is to become dynamic and effective not only in its educational vision, but also in its vision of holistic care. Teachers, students and principals have innate needs to be loved and to love, to be productive and creative, to find their own unique ways of living life and to come to a spiritual place of peacefulness, meaning and fulfilment. Homes and schools need to be environments where such needs are upheld and safeguarded.

The home or school system is only as good as the people in it. Systems have no life without people; when people change, systems change. For example, when principals, teachers, students, school inspectors and Department of Education ministers and officials take on the responsibilities of a philosophy of care, then schools will become the holistic centres of care and education that they need to be. The same holds true for parents, children and childminders in the home and for all members of a community.

❑ *Caring homes*

The first community is the family. Its influence far surpasses the effects of the wider culture on children. The word 'community' comes from the word 'communion', meaning 'union with another'. Rather than a state of *communion* in the family, what often takes place is a *fusion* of family members where there is no separateness, individuality, uniqueness or independence; other families create *diffusion* where there is little, if any, connection between members and where there is no security or launch pad for separateness, individuality and independence. A family that is a real community has strong unity between members, but all members have freedom to be themselves and separateness is endorsed. It promotes connectedness among members and uses this as the foundation to build self-reliance, independence, self-control and the capacity for offspring to fly the nest in early adulthood. The healthy family creates interactions that promote the optimal development of each member of the family.

■ Caring for parents

Who cares for parents? The answer in the first instance is the parents themselves. When there are two parents in the family, then a mutual caring for each other is integral to their relationship. Some partners believe that the relationship is there purely for their benefit and rarely, if ever, identify or respond to the needs of their companion, while other partners believe that the relationship is only there for the other person. Neither situation produces a communion in the relationship.

When a couple are unified but separate they each will assert their own needs and, whenever possible, will be sensitive and responsive to the other's expressed and unexpressed emotional, social, sexual, physical, intellectual, occupational, creative and spiritual needs. They affirm and support each other's unique identity and independence and they see that separateness is the basis for togetherness. When they move on to form a family, they share the responsibilities for child-rearing, whilst maintaining a balanced emphasis on their couple relationship and on their own individual development. As the children grow older, they help them to see that caring is a two-way street and that parents and children both need each other's love and help. They also are firm that siblings show care for each other; this point is missed in many families, and, when it is, siblings can make life very difficult for each other.

It is certainly in the best interests of neighbours, community leaders, educational, social, medical and religious professions and government to be in the forefront of caring for parents. All systems in society are profoundly affected by family systems. Each family is a unique culture and individuals will emerge from it with strengths and weaknesses peculiar to that family. It is unwise to assume that, without systematic intervention, the wider culture will capitalise on the strengths and resolve the weaknesses of these individuals. Creating opportunities for training in parenting, support for besieged parents, respite parenting, counselling for troubled individual parents and couple therapy for partners in conflict not only will benefit parents but will also have positive spin-offs for communities, schools, churches and the country as a whole.

■ Caring for children

In setting up discipline and 'beyond discipline' systems and finding ways to empower their children, parents are already showing considerable caring for their children. But parents have many other responsibilities towards children – emotional, physical, social, sexual, creative and spiritual.

Parents can only care for their children from the well of their own caring for themselves and for each other. Furthermore, parents can only bring their children to the level of personal, interpersonal and spiritual development they have attained themselves. This is why all effective parenting starts with parents firstly learning to care effectively for themselves. Because this can take considerable time to achieve, it is important that, in the meantime, other adults do their utmost to care for children in their community. Loving and caring for children must not be left exclusively to parents.

In order to create harmony in a family, parents need to:

- Unconditionally love self
- Unconditionally love one another
- Take responsibility for self
- Care for each other
- Unconditionally love children
- Know the interactions that raise and lower their own and their children's sense of themselves
- Identify and do their best to respond to the rights and needs of children
- Create a system of fair, firm discipline for all family members
- Foster self-reliance, separateness and independence in themselves and children
- Accept their own vulnerability and show their children how they grow from it
- Withstand undue interference in the family from outside influences
- Resolve problems that threaten family harmony
- Listen to each other and to the children
- Recognise when help is needed and get it

❏ *Caring schools*

The philosophy of a caring school views teachers, students, principals and managers as human beings who have emotional, social, physical, sexual, intellectual, educational, sensual, occupational and spiritual rights and needs, and it does everything in its power to listen and to respond to those needs. The caring school knows that its holistic approach will create the security, safety, challenge and excitement for both teachers and students to embrace the educational aspirations of the school. It knows that valuing and affirming people must always take precedence over teaching and learning. It accepts the profound influence that self-esteem has on teaching and learning and it promotes interactions that raise the self-esteem of teachers, leaders, students and parents. It gives special attention to those who feel bad about themselves and lack self-confidence. It sees the uniqueness, vast worth and endless potential of these individuals and attempts to communicate that image to them. It affirms the enormous intellectual capacity of each of its members and does not confuse knowledge or skill with intellectual potential. It embraces failure and success as equal stepping-stones in the wonderful process of learning and, most of all, praises efforts to learn and encourages a love of learning. It seeks to avoid making either teaching or learning a threat to anyone's welfare. It sees the pitfalls in emphasising academic performance, examination results, competition and public comparisons among students and teachers. It puts great stress on caring relationships between all members of the school and does not tolerate any disrespect of any member of the school. It recognises the vulnerabilities of managers, teachers and students and creates a confidential welfare service for distressed members. It is concerned for those teachers who are stressed and have lost their love of teaching, and it offers opportunities for personal and professional growth and change. It is equally mindful of those students who lose motivation and seeks ways to rekindle their innate eagerness to learn. It promotes a person-centred rather than a programme-centred educational approach. The caring school reaches out with heart and mind to its members and sees an effective discipline system as integral to its caring.

■ Caring for teachers

The most valuable asset a school has is its staff. Schools need to take care of their teachers and leaders and to ensure that their work does not become more important than their worth. Regrettably, this is precisely what seems to have happened and, as a result, the physical and emotional welfare of many teachers is at risk. This imbalance has to be redressed, firstly, because teachers deserve care, and secondly, to stop the exit of effective teachers from the educational system and make the profession more attractive to young aspirants.

Caring does not mean taking responsibility for people. What it does mean is communicating directly and clearly, sincere and active listening, responsiveness to reasonable needs, and the presence of support and help when people are struggling.

Whether schools like it or not, teachers come into the job with a wide range of needs and if these are ignored, dismissed or neglected, the teacher's motivation to work and cooperate with job demands will be negatively affected. Whilst each teacher will have some needs unique to her, there are needs that are common to all teachers. Deeper caring lies in identifying and being empathic to the unique needs of teachers.

Needs of teachers	
• Physical needs	Health • energy • heat • comfort • ease • nutritious food • safety from physical threats • care of personal property
• Emotional needs	To receive and give love • respect • affirmation of uniqueness • freedom and safety to express both welfare and emergency feelings • support • empathy • compassion
• Social needs	Significance given to presence in and absence from school • direct and clear communication • inclusion in decision-making • equal affirmation of specialness • acknowledgment of work contributions • social outings with colleagues • group problem-solving • high level of staff involvement • leaders and colleagues to be available and ⟶

	approachable • back-up support when discipline problems arise • absence of comparisons with other teachers • failures and successes not to be measures of their worth • safety to admit coping difficulties • help • confidentiality
• Intellectual needs	Affirmation of intellectual potential • equal valuing of all teaching subjects • opinions and innovativeness to be given due hearing • evaluation through teaching efforts and not students' academic performance • entitlement to own philosophies and view-points • non-conformity • ongoing professional development and education
• Sensual needs	Sensitivity to their individual tastes in food • art • literature • music • sports • architecture • interior design • dress sense • colour preference
• Sexual needs	Own sexual orientation • freedom from sexual harassment or innuendo • freedom to maintain own views on sexual education
• Occupational needs	Physical, emotional, social, intellectual and sexual safety at work • fair treatment • consultation • opportunities for promotion • ongoing training • time and resources for further education
• Creative needs	Acceptance of difference • affirmation of own unique and creative way of living and teaching • freedom to be innovative • freedom to express ideas different to majority
• Spiritual needs	Respect for own religious or spiritual orientation • freedom to say 'no' to teaching religion if it is contrary to own beliefs

■ Caring for students

It is the relationships with teachers and principal that largely determine whether students enjoy being in class and school. In my work with students who have difficulties in school, the main complaint is their treatment by teachers. Many feel misunderstood, not listened to, 'put down', not liked, not important, 'less than' other students and uncared for by teachers. This is not to say that these students did not have their own inner difficulties, but the nature of their teachers' relationships with them exacerbated how they already felt about themselves. It also confirmed their worst fears that adults do not care. Being warm and caring towards students does not in any way mean having to tolerate difficult behaviours. It does mean vindicating rights in a way that does not jeopardise the relationship with the student or lower his self-esteem. The mature teacher apologises quickly when she loses control, so that the rift in the relationship with the student is healed and the discipline matter is resolved without further loss of face for either teacher or student.

The needs of students are very similar to those of teachers. Suffice it to say here that caring for students involves:

- Seeing the person of the student as infinitely more important than his schoolwork or any misconduct
- Viewing the relationship with the student as sacred and not allowing any behaviour to jeopardise it
- Acknowledging that how the student learns is directly related to how he sees himself
- Finding ways to develop relationships with students in and out of class
- Being available and approachable
- Not being afraid to show vulnerability
- Correcting difficult behaviours in a way that emphasises the teacher's own rights and needs and is not punishing
- Making students' presence and absence positively felt
- Involving students in decision-making, project development and care for other students
- Putting emphasis on educational effort rather than academic performance
- Responding to mistakes and failures as gems in the crown of learning
- Viewing success and failure as relative terms
- Giving students a sense of their enormous intellectual capacity

- Not confusing knowledge and intelligence
- Ensuring learning has only positive associations
- Apologising when control is lost
- Requesting rather than commanding
- Being person-centred rather than programme-centred
- Being fair, consistent and predictable in response to disruptive behaviours
- Showing concern for undisciplined students (whether over-controlled or under-controlled)
- Listening to students

■ Caring for parents

I believe that every school should have a special space which parents feel is their own and where they feel free to drop in at will. It is important that this room is well-decorated, well-equipped and comfortable and is used exclusively by and for parents. Parents must be involved directly in decisions about its use and maintenance.

How teachers and the school principal relate to parents is the real benchmark of whether or not caring for parents is promoted in the school. Parents deserve respect at all times and active listening to their opinions and concerns. Teachers need to ensure that arrangements to meet parents are flexible and they need to be sensitive to the nervousness some parents experience coming in to the school. Parents need to be involved in the school on the basis of equal and complementary status with teachers. This implies the sharing of information, responsibility, decision-making, problem-solving and account-ability. The danger of involving only those parents who are already knowledgeable and self-confident about themselves, their children and education must be avoided. It will be necessary to formulate special means of involving parents who, because of their own poor education, poor self-esteem, family poverty or bad school experiences, are reluctant to participate.

Along with emotional and social needs to be valued and included, parents also have educational needs which the school could meet as part of its caring programme for parents. Educational activities that schools could organise, or cooperate with others on organising, are parenting courses, relationship courses, workshops on children's homework and the school curriculum, leisure activities (for example, arts and crafts, swimming, yoga, drama), self-development courses (for example, stress management, communication, assertiveness, relaxation, self-esteem), home management programmes (for example, cookery, gardening, budgeting, interior decoration, first aid), second chance education (for example, literacy, numeracy, Leaving Certificate, other certificate and diploma courses), leadership training and community education.

The inclusion of parents as equal and complementary partners in the education of their children also entails keeping parents informed of school practices. This is a two-way process as teachers need information from parents about their children's educational progress or lack of it. Open days, regular parent–teacher meetings, consultation on discipline systems and use of parents' ideas on creative developments for the school are some ways of setting up a two-way flow of information. Teachers need to bow to the fact that parents know more about their children and they need to avail of this knowledge.

Parents can be invaluable for fundraising, helping with sports, plays, concerts and other extracurricular activities, and accompanying teachers on educational tours and other outings.

Joint activities would enhance the presence of parents in the school. Teachers and parents can do training programmes together. Parents can work voluntarily as classroom assistants, can supervise students sent to the sanction room, can be members of working parties on aspects of the school development plan and can play a part in the production of classroom materials.

Parents too are probably the best envoys to reach out to those parents who are reluctant to be involved in the school. Very often, parents who are reluctant to participate in the school are the ones who need the most caring, training, self-development, family support and help.

In accepting and being respectful of parents, in being sensitive and compassionate to their vulnerability when their children are being troublesome and in listening to their side of the story, teachers meet the emotional needs of parents in relation to the school. In involving them in school development, in consulting them on their children's overall welfare in the school and in socialising with them, teachers are responsive to the social needs of parents. In organising, recruiting and encouraging them in parent training, personal development and further education, the school is meeting the intellectual and educational needs of parents. Teachers can do much to enhance many aspects of parents' personal and family development, and in doing so prepare the ground for effective partnership with them.